M000198310

Selected Poems

GILLIAN CLARKE, National Poet for Wales since 2008, was born in Cardiff and lives in Ceredigion. She is President of Tŷ Newydd, the Welsh Writers' Centre which she co-founded in 1990. She has published ten collections of poems and a book of prose, *At the Source*. Her latest poetry collection, *Ice*, was shortlisted for the TS Eliot Award. In December 2010 she was awarded the Queen's Gold Medal for Poetry, and the Wilfred Owen Award in 2012.

Gillian Clarke

Selected Poems

PICADOR

First published 2016 by Picador
an imprint of Pan Macmillan
20 New Wharf Road, London N1 9RR
Associated companies throughout the world
www.panmacmillan.com

ISBN 978-1-5098-2192-1

3 5 7 9 8 6 4 2

A CIP catalogue record for this book is available from the British Library.

Printed and bound by CPI Group (UK) Ltd, Croydon CR0 4YY

For Catrin, Owain and Dylan

Contents

The Sundial 1

Blaen Cwrt 2

Baby-Sitting 4

Lunchtime Lecture 5

Last Rites 7

Catrin 8

Letter from a Far Country 10

Miracle on St David's Day 26

Llŷr 28

Siege 30

The Water-Diviner 33

Plums 34

October 36

At One Thousand Feet 37

Neighbours 38

Storm 40

Seal 41

Ichthyosaur 42

Cold Knap Lake 43

Apples   44

Oranges   45

Talking of Burnings in Walter Savage Landor's Smithy   46

Marged   48

My Box   49

The Hare   50

February   53

Peregrine Falcon   54

Wil Williams (1861–1910)   55

Annie (1868–1944)   56

The King of Britain's Daughter   57

Radio Engineer   62

Musician   65

Anorexic   66

The Vet   68

Lament   69

The Field-Mouse   70

Ark   71

A Difficult Birth, Easter 1998   73

Architect   74

Glass   75

Amber   79

The White Ship   80

The Lace-Maker   82

Women's Work   83

Snow   84

Into the Mountain   85

The Paddle Steamers   88

Voicing the Organ   89

Sloes   91

Translation   93

In the Beginning   94

Mother Tongue   95

The Fisherman   96

The Piano   97

Erik Satie and the Blackbird   98

RS   100

The Stone Poems   101

Nine Green Gardens   109

Breathing   115

On the Train   116

Making the Beds for the Dead   117

Aftermath 125

Flood 126

First Words 127

A Pocket Dictionary 128

Not 129

Otter 130

The Fox and the Girl 131

Nettles 132

A Recipe for Water 133

A Barge on the Severn 136

Glacier 143

Coins 144

Llandâf Cathedral 145

A Sonnet for Nye 146

Mercury 147

Bach at St Davids 148

Wings 149

Old Libraries 150

Advent 151

Dawn 152

Polar 153

Ice   154

River   155

Snow   156

White Nights   157

Freeze 1947   158

Swans   159

Who Killed the Swan?   160

Thaw   161

Fluent   162

Nant Mill   163

Burnet Moths   164

Er Gwell, Er Gwaeth   165

Running Away to the Sea – 1955   166

Oradour, 10 June 1944   167

Six Bells   168

Blue Hydrangeas   169

The March   170

The Year's Midnight   172

The Sundial

Owain was ill today. In the night
He was delirious, shouting of lions
In the sleepless heat. Today, dry
And pale, he took a paper circle,
Laid it on the grass which held it
With curling fingers. In the still
Centre he pushed the broken bean
Stick, gathering twelve fragments
Of stone, placed them at measured
Distances. Then he crouched, slightly
Trembling with fever, calculating
The mathematics of sunshine.

He looked up, his eyes dark,
Intelligently adult as though
The wave of fever taught silence
And immobility for the first time.
Here, in his enforced rest, he found
Deliberation, and the slow finger
Of light, quieter than night lions,
More worthy of his concentration.
All day he told the time to me.
All day we felt and watched the sun
Caged in its white diurnal heat,
Pointing at us with its black stick.

Blaen Cwrt

You ask how it is. I will tell you.
There is no glass. The air spins in
The stone rectangle. We warm our hands
With apple wood. Some of the smoke
Rises against the ploughed, brown field
As a sign to our neighbours in the
Four folds of the valley that we are in.
Some of the smoke seeps through the stones
Into the barn where it curls like fern
On the walls. Holding a thick root
I press my bucket through the surface
Of the water, lift it brimming and skim
The leaves away. Our fingers curl on
Enamel mugs of tea, like ploughmen.
The stones clear in the rain
Giving their colours. It's not easy.
There are no brochure blues or boiled sweet
Reds. All is ochre and earth and cloud-green
Nettles tasting sour and the smells of moist
Earth and sheep's wool. The wattle and daub
Chimney hood has decayed away, slowly
Creeping to dust, chalking the slate
Floor with stories. It has all the first
Necessities for a high standard
Of civilised living: silence inside
A circle of sound, water and fire,
Light on uncountable miles of mountain

From a big, unpredictable sky,
Two rooms, waking and sleeping,
Two languages, two centuries of past
To ponder on, and the basic need
To work hard in order to survive.

Baby-sitting

I am sitting in a strange room listening
For the wrong baby. I don't love
This baby. She is sleeping a snuffly
Roseate, bubbling sleep; she is fair;
She is a perfectly acceptable child.
I am afraid of her. If she wakes
She will hate me. She will shout
Her hot midnight rage, her nose
Will stream disgustingly and the perfume
Of her breath will fail to enchant me.

To her I will represent absolute
Abandonment. For her it will be worse
Than for the lover cold in lonely
Sheets; worse than for the woman who waits
A moment to collect her dignity
Beside the bleached bone in the terminal ward.
As she rises sobbing from the monstrous land
Stretching for milk-familiar comforting,
She will find me and between us two
It will not come. It will not come.

Lunchtime Lecture

And this from the second or third millennium
B.C., a female, aged about twenty-two.
A white, fine skull, full up with darkness
As a shell with sea, drowned in the centuries.
Small, perfect. The cranium would fit the palm
Of a man's hand. Some plague or violence
Destroyed her, and her whiteness lay safe in a shroud
Of silence, undisturbed, unrained on, dark
For four thousand years. Till a tractor in summer
Biting its way through the longcairn for supplies
Of stone, broke open the grave and let a crowd of light
Stare in at her, and she stared quietly back.

As I look at her I feel none of the shock
The farmer felt as, unprepared, he found her.
Here in the Museum, like death in hospital,
Reasons are given, labels, causes, catalogues.
The smell of death is done. Left, only her bone
Purity, the light and shade beauty that her man
Was denied sight of, the perfect edge of the place
Where the pieces join, with no mistakes, like boundaries.

She's a tree in winter, stripped white on a black sky,
Leafless formality, brow, bough in fine relief.
I, at some other season, illustrate the tree
Fleshed, with woman's hair and colours and the rustling
Blood, the troubled mind that she has overthrown.

We stare at each other, dark into sightless
Dark, seeing only ourselves in the black pools,
Gulping the risen sea that booms in the shell.

Last Rites

During this summer of the long drought
The road to Synod Inn has kept
Its stigmata of dust and barley-seed;

At the inquest they tell it again:
How the lorry tents us from the sun,
His pulse dangerous in my hands,
A mains hum only, no message
Coming through. His face warm, profiled
Against tarmac, the two-stroke Yamaha
Dead as a black horse in a war.
Only his hair moves and the sound
Of the parched grass and harebells a handspan
Away, his fear still with me like the scream
Of a jet in an empty sky.
I cover him with the grey blanket
From my bed, touch his face as a child
Who makes her favourite cosy.
His blood on my hands, his cariad* in my arms.

Driving her home we share that vision
Over August fields dying of drought
Of the summer seas shattering
At every turn of Cardigan Bay
Under the cruel stones of the sun.

* Cariad: darling (Welsh)

[7]

Catrin

I can remember you, child,
As I stood in a hot, white
Room at the window watching
The people and cars taking
Turn at the traffic lights.
I can remember you, our first
Fierce confrontation, the tight
Red rope of love which we both
Fought over. It was a square
Environmental blank, disinfected
Of paintings or toys. I wrote
All over the walls with my
Words, coloured the clean squares
With the wild, tender circles
Of our struggle to become
Separate. We want, we shouted,
To be two, to be ourselves.

Neither won nor lost the struggle
In the glass tank clouded with feelings
Which changed us both. Still I am fighting
You off, as you stand there
With your straight, strong, long
Brown hair and your rosy,
Defiant glare, bringing up
From the heart's pool that old rope,
Tightening about my life,

Trailing love and conflict,
As you ask may you skate
In the dark, for one more hour.

Letter from a Far Country

They have gone. The silence resettles
slowly as dust on the sunlit
surfaces of the furniture.
At first the skull itself makes
sounds in any fresh silence,
a big sea running in a shell.
I can hear my blood rise and fall.

Dear husbands, fathers, forefathers,
this is my apologia, my
letter home from the future,
my bottle in the sea which might
take a generation to arrive.

The morning's all activity.
I draw the detritus of a family's
loud life before me, a snow plough,
a road-sweeper with my cart of leaves.
The washing-machine drones
in the distance. From time to time
as it falls silent I fill baskets
with damp clothes and carry them
into the garden, hang them out,
stand back, take pleasure counting
and listing what I have done.
The furniture is brisk with polish.
On the shelves in all of the rooms

I arrange the books
in alphabetical order
according to subject: Mozart,
Advanced Calculus, William
and Paddington Bear.
Into the drawers I place your clean
clothes, pyjamas with buttons
sewn back on, shirts stacked neatly
under their labels on the shelves.

The chests and cupboards are full,
the house sweet as a honeycomb.
I move in and out of the hive
all day, harvesting, ordering.
You will find all in its proper place,
when I have gone.

As I write I am far away.
First see a landscape. Hill country,
essentially feminine,
the sea not far off. Bryn Isaf
down there in the crook of the hill
under Calfaria's single eye.
My grandmother might have lived there.
Any farm. Any chapel.
Father and minister, on guard,
close the white gates to hold her.

A stony track turns between
ancient hedges, narrowing,
like a lane in a child's book.

Its perspective makes the heart restless
like the boy in the rhyme, his stick
and cotton bundle on his shoulder.

The minstrel boy to the war has gone.
But the girl stays. To mind things.
She must keep. And wait. And pass time.

There's always been time on our hands.
We read this perfectly white page
for the black head of the seal,
for the cormorant, as suddenly gone
as a question from the mind,
snaking underneath the surfaces.
A cross of gull shadow on the sea
as if someone stepped on its grave.
After an immeasurable space
the cormorant breaks the surface
as a small, black, returning doubt.

From here the valley is narrow,
the lane lodged like a halfway ledge.
From the opposite wood the birds
ring like a tambourine. It's not
the birdsong of a garden, thrush
and blackbird, robin and finch,
distinguishable, taking turn.
The song's lost in saps and seepings,
amplified by hollow trees,
cupped leaves and wind in the branches.
All their old conversations

collected carefully, faded
and difficult to read, yet held
forever as voices in a well.

Reflections and fallen stones; shouts
into the scared dark of lead-mines;
the ruined warehouse where the owls stare;
sea-caves; cellars; the back stairs
behind the chenille curtain;
the landing when the lights are out;
nightmares in hot feather beds;
the barn where I'm sent to fetch Taid*;
that place where the Mellte flows
boldly into limestone caves
and leaps from its hole a mile on,
the nightmare still wild in its voice.

When I was a child a young boy
was drawn into a pipe and drowned
at the swimming pool. I never
forgot him, and pity rivers
inside mountains, and the children
of Hamlyn sucked in by music.
You can hear children crying
from the empty woods.
It's all given back in concert
with the birds and leaves and water
and the song and dance of the Piper.

* Taid: grandfather (North Wales)

Listen! to the starlings glistening
on a March morning! Just one day
after snow, an hour after frost,
the thickening grass begins to shine
already in the opening light.
There's wind to rustle the blood,
the sudden flame of crocus.

My grandmother might be standing
in the great silence before the Wars,
hanging the washing between trees
over the white and the red hens.
Sheets. Threadworked pillowcases.
Mamgu's* best pais†. Her Sunday frock.

The sea stirs restlessly between
the sweetness of clean sheets,
the lifted arms,
the rustling petticoats.

My mother's laundry list, ready
on Mondays when the van called.
The rest soaked in glutinous starch
and whitened with a bluebag
kept in a broken cup.

---

* Mamgu: grandmother (South Wales)
† Pais: petticoat (Welsh)

(In the airing cupboard you'll see
a map, numbering and placing
every towel, every sheet.
I have charted all your needs.)

It has always been a matter
of lists. We have been counting,
folding, measuring, making,
tenderly laundering cloth
ever since we have been women.

The waves are folded meticulously,
perfectly white. Then they are tumbled
and must come to be folded again.

Four herring gulls and their shadows
are shouting at the clear glass
of a shaken wave. The sea's a sheet
bellying in the wind, snapping.
Air and white linen. Our airing cupboards
are full of our satisfactions.

The gulls grieve at our contentment.
It is a masculine question.
'Where' they call 'are your great works?'
They slip their fetters and fly up
to laugh at land-locked women.
Their cries are cruel as greedy babies.

Our milky tendernesses dry
to crisp lists; immaculate
linen; jars labelled and glossy
with our perfect preserves.
Spiced oranges; green tomato
chutney; Seville orange marmalade
annually staining gold
the snows of January.

(The saucers of marmalade
are set when the amber wrinkles
like the sea if you blow it.)

Jams and jellies of blackberry,
crabapple, strawberry, plum,
greengage and loganberry.
You can see the fruit pressing
their little faces against the glass;
tiny onions imprisoned
in their preservative juices.

Familiar days are stored whole
in bottles. There's a wet morning
orchard in the dandelion wine;
a white spring distilled
in elderflower's clarity;
and a loving, late, sunburning
day of October in syrups
of rose hip and the beautiful
black sloes that stained the gin to rose.

It is easy to make of love
these ceremonials. As priests
we fold cloth, break bread, share wine,
hope there's enough to go round.

(You'll find my inventories pinned
inside all of the cupboard doors.)

Soon they'll be planting the barley.
I imagine I see it, stirring
like blown sand, feel the stubble
cutting my legs above blancoed
daps in a summer too hot
for Wellingtons. The cans of tea
swing squeakily on wire loops,
outheld, not to scald myself,
over the ten slow leagues
of the field of golden knives.
To be out with the men, at work,
I had longed to carry their tea,
for the feminine privilege,
for the male right to the field.
Even that small task made me bleed.
Halfway between the flowered lap
of my grandmother and the black
heraldic silhouette of men
and machines on the golden field,
I stood crying, my ankle bones
raw and bleeding like the poppies
trussed in the corn stooks in their torn
red silks and soft mascara blacks.

(The recipe for my best bread,
half granary meal, half strong brown flour,
water, sugar, yeast and salt,
is copied out in the small black book.)

In the black book of this parish
a hundred years ago
you will find the unsupported
woman had 'pauper' against her name.
She shared it with old men.
The parish was rich with movement.
The woollen mills were spinning.
Water-wheels milled the sunlight
and the loom's knock was a heart
behind all activity.
The shuttles were quick as birds
in the warp of the oakwoods.
In the fields the knives were out
in a glint of husbandry.
In back bedrooms, barns and hedges,
in hollows of the hills,
the numerous young were born.

The people were at work:
dressmaker; wool carder; quilter;
midwife; farmer; apprentice;
house servant; scholar; labourer;
shepherd; stocking knitter; tailor;
carpenter; mariner; ploughman;
wool spinner; cobbler; cottager;
Independent Minister.

And the paupers: Enoch Elias
and Ann, his wife; David Jones,
Sarah and Esther their daughter;
Mary Evans and Ann Tanrallt;
Annie Cwm March and child;
Eleanor Thomas, widow, Crug Glas;
Sara Jones, 84, and daughter;
Nicholas Rees, aged 80, and his wife;
Mariah Evans the Cwm, widow;
on the parish for want of work.
Housebound by infirmity, age,
widowhood, or motherhood.
Before the Welfare State who cared
for sparrows in a hard spring?

The stream's cleaner now; it idles
past derelict mill-wheels; the drains
do its work. Since the tanker sank
the unfolding rose of the sea
blooms on the beaches, wave on wave
black, track-marked, each tide
a procession of the dead.
Slack water's treacherous; each veined
wave is a stain in seal-milk;
the sea gapes, hopelessly
licking itself.

(Examine your hands
scrupulously
for signs of dirt in your own blood.
And wash them before meals.)

In that innocent smallholding
where the swallows live and field mice
winter and the sheep barge in
under the browbone, the windows
are blind, are doors for owls,
bolt-holes for dreams. The thoughts have flown.
The last death was a suicide.
The lowing cows discovered her,
the passing-bell of their need
warned a winter morning that day
when no one came to milk them.
Later, they told me, a baby
was born in the room where she died,
as if by this means sanctified,
a death outcried by a birth.
Middle-aged, poor, isolated,
she could not recover
from mourning an old parent's death.
Influenza brought an hour
too black, too narrow to escape.

More mysterious to them
was the woman who had everything.
A village house with railings;
rooms of good furniture;
fine linen in the drawers;
a garden full of herbs and flowers;
a husband in work; grown sons.
She had a cloud on her mind,

they said, and her death shadowed them.
It couldn't be explained.

I watch for her face looking out,
small and white, from every window,
like a face in a jar. Gossip,
whispers, lowing sounds. Laughter.

The people have always talked.
The landscape collects conversations
as carefully as a bucket,
gives them back in concert
with a wood of birdsong.

(If you hear your name in that talk
don't listen. Eavesdroppers never
heard anything good of themselves.)

When least expected you catch
the eye of the enemy
looking coldly from the old world . . .
Here's a woman who ought to be
up to her wrists in marriage;
not content with the second hand
she is shaking the bracelets
from her arms. The sea circles
her ankles. Watch its knots loosen
from the delicate bones
of her feet, from the rope of foam
about a rock. The seal swims

in a collar of water
drawing the horizon in its wake.
And doubt breaks the perfect
white surface of the day.

About the tree in the middle
of the cornfield the loop of gold
is loose as water; as the love
we should bear one another.

When I rock the sea rocks. The moon
doesn't seem to be listening
invisible in a pale sky,
keeping a light hand on the rein.

Where is woman in this trinity?
The mare who draws the load?
The hand on the leather?
The cargo of wheat?

Watching sea-roads I feel
the tightening white currents,
am waterlogged, my time set
to the sea's town clock.
My cramps and drownings, energies,
desires draw the loaded net
of the tide over the stones.

A lap full of pebbles and then
light as a Coca Cola can.

I am freight. I am ship.
I cast ballast overboard.
The moon decides my Equinox.
At high tide I am leaving.

The women are leaving.
They are paying their taxes
and dues. Filling in their passports.
They are paying to Caesar
what is Caesar's, to God what is God's,
To Woman what is Man's.

I hear the dead grandmothers,
Mamgu from Ceredigion,
Nain* from the North, all calling
their daughters down from the fields,
calling me in from the road.
They haul at the taut silk cords;
set us fetching eggs, feeding hens,
mixing rage with the family bread,
lock us to the elbows in soap suds.
Their sculleries and kitchens fill
with steam, sweetnesses, goosefeathers.

On the graves of my grandfathers
the stones, in their lichens and mosses,
record each one's importance.

* Nain: grandmother (North Wales)

Diaconydd*. Trysorydd†.
Pillars of their society.
Three times at chapel on Sundays.
They are in league with the moon
but as silently stony
as the simple names of their women.

We are hawks trained to return
to the lure from the circle's
far circumference. Children sing
that note that only we can hear.
The baby breaks the waters,
disorders the blood's tune, sets
each filament of the senses
wild. Its cry tugs at flesh, floods
its mother's milky fields.
Nightly in white moonlight I wake
from sleep one whole slow minute
before the hungry child
wondering what woke me.

School's out. The clocks strike four.
Today this letter goes unsigned,
unfinished, unposted.
When it is finished
I will post it from a far country.

*

* Diaconydd: deacon
† Trysorydd: treasurer

If we launch the boat and sail away
Who will rock the cradle? Who will stay?
If women wander over the sea
Who'll be home when you come in for tea?

If we go hunting along with the men
Who will light the fires and bake bread then?
Who'll catch the nightmares and ride them away
If we put to sea and we sail away?

Will the men grow tender and the children strong?
Who will teach the Mam iaith and sing them songs?
If we adventure more than a day
Who will do the loving while we're away?

Miracle on St David's Day

'They flash upon that inward eye
Which is the bliss of solitude'
  – 'The Daffodils' by W. Wordsworth

An afternoon yellow and open-mouthed
with daffodils. The sun treads the path
among cedars and enormous oaks.
It might be a country house, guests strolling,
the rumps of gardeners between nursery shrubs.

I am reading poetry to the insane.
An old woman, interrupting, offers
as many buckets of coal as I need.
A beautiful chestnut-haired boy listens
entirely absorbed. A schizophrenic

on a good day, they tell me later.
In a cage of first March sun a woman
sits not listening, not seeing, not feeling.
In her neat clothes the woman is absent.
A big, mild man is tenderly led

to his chair. He has never spoken.
His labourer's hands on his knees, he rocks
gently to the rhythms of the poems.
I read to their presences, absences,
to the big, dumb labouring man as he rocks.

He is suddenly standing, silently,
huge and mild, but I feel afraid. Like slow
movement of spring water or the first bird
of the year in the breaking darkness,
the labourer's voice recites 'The Daffodils'.

The nurses are frozen, alert; the patients
seem to listen. He is hoarse but word-perfect.
Outside the daffodils are still as wax,
a thousand, ten thousand, their syllables
unspoken, their creams and yellows still.

Forty years ago, in a Valleys school,
the class recited poetry by rote.
Since the dumbness of misery fell
he has remembered there was a music
of speech and that once he had something to say.

When he's done, before the applause, we observe
the flowers' silence. A thrush sings
and the daffodils are flame.

Llŷr

Ten years old, at my first Stratford play:
The river* and the king† with their Welsh names
Bore in the darkness of a summer night
Through interval and act and interval.
Swans moved double through glossy water
Gleaming with imponderable meanings.
Was it Gielgud on that occasion?
Or ample Laughton, crazily white-gowned,
Pillowed in wheatsheaves on a wooden cart,
Who taught the significance of little words?
All. Nothing. Fond. Ingratitude. Words
To keep me scared, awake at night. That old
Man's vanity and a daughter's 'Nothing',
Ran like a nursery rhyme in my head.

Thirty years later on the cliffs of Llŷn‡
I watch how Edgar's crows and choughs still measure
How high cliffs are, how thrown stones fall
Into history, how deeply the bruise
Spreads in the sea where the wave has broken.
The turf is stitched with tormentil and thrift,
Blue squill and bird bones, tiny shells, heartsease.
Yellowhammers sing like sparks in the gorse.

* Avon/afon: river (Welsh)
† Llŷr: Lear
‡ Llŷn: N.W. Peninsula of Wales

The landscape's marked with figures of old men:
The bearded sea; thin-boned, wind-bent trees;
Shepherd and labourer and night-fisherman.
Here and there among the crumbling farms
Are lit kitchen windows on distant hills,
And guilty daughters longing to be gone.

Night falls on Llŷn, on forefathers,
Old Celtic kings and the more recent dead,
Those we are still guilty about, flowers
Fade in jam jars on their graves; renewed
Refusals are heavy on our minds.
My head is full of sound, remembered speech,
Syllables, ideas just out of reach;
The close, looped sound of curlew and the far
Subsidiary roar, cadences shaped
By the long coast of the peninsula,
The continuous pentameter of the sea.
When I was ten a fool and a king sang
Rhymes about sorrow, and there I heard
That nothing is until it has a word.

Siege

I waste the sun's last hour, sitting here
at the kitchen window. Tea and a pile
of photographs to sort. Radio news
like smoke of conflagrations far away.
There isn't room for another petal
or leaf out there, this year of blossom.
Light dazzles the hedge roots underneath
the heavy shadows, burns the long grass.

I, in my father's arms in this garden
with dandelion hair. He, near forty,
unaccustomed to the restlessness
of a baby's energy. Small hands
tear apart the photograph's composure.
She pushes his chest to be let down
where daisies embroider his new shoes.

Perfumes and thorns are tearing
from the red may tree. Wild white morello
and a weeping cherry heavy in flower.
The lilac slowly shows. Small oaks spread
their gestures. Poplars glisten. Pleated green
splits black husks of ash. Magnolia
drops its wax. Forsythia
fallen like a yellow dress.
Underfoot daisies from a deep
original root burst the darkness.

My mother, posing in a summer dress
in the corn at harvest time. Her brothers,
shadowy middle distance figures,
stoop with pitchforks to lift the sheaves.
Out of sight Captain, or Belle, head fallen
to rest in the lee of the load, patient
for the signal. Out of heart too the scare
of the field far down from the sunstruck top
of the load, and the lurch at the gate
as we ditch and sway left down the lane.

The fallen sun lies low in the bluebells.
It is nearly summer. Midges hang
in the air. A wren is singing, sweet
in a lilac tree. Thrushes hunt the lawn,
eavesdrop for stirrings in the daisy roots.
The wren repeats her message distantly,
In a race of speedwell over grass
the thrushes are silently listening.
A yellow butterfly begins
its unsteady journey over the lawn.

The radio voices break and suddenly
the garden burns, is full of barking dogs.
A woman screams and gunsmoke blossoms
in the apple trees. Sheaves of fire
are scorching the grass and in my kitchen
is a roar of floors falling, machine guns.

The wren moves closer and repeats that song
of lust and burgeoning. Never clearer
the figures standing on the lawn, sharpnesses
of a yellow butterfly, almost there.

The Water-Diviner

His fingers tell water like prayer.
He hears its voice in the silence
through fifty feet of rock
on an afternoon dumb with drought.

Under an old tin bath, a stone,
an upturned can, his copper pipe
glints with discovery. We dip our hose
deep into the dark, sucking its dryness,

till suddenly the water answers,
not the little sound we know,
but a thorough bass too deep
for the naked ear, shouts through the hose

a word we could not say, or spell, or remember,
something like 'dŵr . . . dŵr'*.

---

* Dŵr: water (Welsh)

Plums

When their time comes they fall
without wind, without rain.
They seep through the trees' muslin
in a slow fermentation.

Daily the low sun warms them
in a late love that is sweeter
than summer. In bed at night
we hear heartbeat of fruitfall.

The secretive slugs crawl home
to the burst honeys, are found
in the morning mouth on mouth,
inseparable.

We spread patchwork counterpanes
for a clean catch. Baskets fill,
never before such harvest,
such a hunters' moon burning

the hawthorns, drunk on syrups
that are richer by night
when spiders pitch
tents in the wet grass.

This morning the red sun
is opening like a rose
on our white wall, prints there
the fishbone shadow of a fern.

The early blackbirds fly
guilty from a dawn haul
of fallen fruit. We too
breakfast on sweetnesses.

Soon plum trees will be bone,
grown delicate with frost's
formalities. Their black
angles will tear the snow.

October

Wind in the poplars and a broken branch,
a dead arm in the bright trees. Five poplars
tremble gradually to gold. The stone face
of the lion darkens in a sharp shower,
his dreadlocks of lobelia grown long,
tangled, more brown now than blue-eyed.

My friend dead and the graveyard at Orcop –
her short ride to the hawthorn hedge, lighter
than hare-bones on men's shoulders, our faces
stony, rain, weeping in the air. The grave
deep as a well takes the earth's thud, the slow
fall of flowers.

        Over the page the pen
runs faster than wind's white steps over grass.
For a while health feels like pain. Then panic
running the fields, the grass, the racing leaves
ahead of light, holding that robin's eye
in the laurel, hydrangeas' faded green.
I must write like the wind, year after year
passing my death-day, winning ground.

At One Thousand Feet

Nobody comes but the postman
and the farmer with winter fodder.

A-road and motorway avoid me.
The national grid has left me out.

For power I catch wind.
In my garden clear water rises.

A wind spinning the blades
of the mill to blinding silver

lets in the rumour,
grief on the radio.

America telephones.
A postcard comes from Poland.

In the sling of its speed the comet
flowers to perihelion over the chimney.

I hold the sky to my ear to hear
pandemonium whispering.

Neighbours

That spring was late. We watched the sky
and studied charts for shouldering isobars.
Birds were late to pair. Crows drank from the lamb's eye.

Over Finland small birds fell: song-thrushes
steering north, smudged signatures on light,
migrating warblers, nightingales.

Wing-beats failed over fjords, each lung a sip of gall.
Children were warned of their dangerous beauty.
Milk was spilt in Poland. Each quarrel

the blowback from some old story,
a mouthful of bitter air from the Ukraine
brought by the wind out of its box of sorrows.

This spring a lamb sips caesium on a Welsh hill.
A child, lifting her face to drink the rain,
takes into her blood the poisoned arrow.

Now we are all neighbourly, each little town
in Europe twinned to Chernobyl, each heart
with the burnt fireman, the child on the Moscow train.

In the democracy of the virus and the toxin
we wait. We watch for bird migrations,
one bird returning with green in its voice,

glasnost
golau glas,*
a first break of blue.

* golau glas: blue light

Storm

The cat lies low, too scared
to cross the garden.

For two days we are bowed
by a whiplash of hurricane.

The hill's a wind-harp.
Our bones are flutes of ice.

The heart drums in its small room
and the river rattles its pebbles.

Thistlefields are comb and paper
whisperings of syllable and bone

till no word's left
but thud and rumble of

something with hooves or wheels,
something breathing too hard.

Seal

When the milk-arrow stabs she comes
water-fluent down the long green miles.
Her milk leaks into the sea, blue
blossoming in an opal.

The pup lies patient in his cot of stone.
They meet with cries, caress as people do.
She lies down for his suckling, lifts him
with a flipper from the sea's reach
when the tide fills his throat with salt.

This is the fourteenth day. In two days
no bitch-head will break the brilliance
listening for baby-cries.
Down in the thunder of that other country
the bulls are calling and her uterus is empty.

Alone and hungering in his fallen shawl
he'll nuzzle the Atlantic and be gone.
If that day's still his moult will lie
a gleaming ring on sand
like the noose she slips on the sea.

Ichthyosaur

at the exhibition of Dinosaurs from China

Jurassic travellers
trailing a wake of ammonites.
Vertebrae swirl in stone's currents,
the broken flotilla of a pilgrimage.
Bone-pods open their secret marrow.

Behind glass she dies, birth-giving.
Millions of years too late it can still move us,
the dolphin-flip of her spine
and the frozen baby turning its head
to the world at the last moment
as all babies do,
drowned as it learned to live.

Small obstetric tragedy,
like a lamb at a field-edge
the wrong way up or strangled at birth
by the mothering cord.
Perhaps earth heaved, slapped a burning hand
on both of them as he ducked under her lintel,
leaving only a grace of bones
eloquent as a word in stone.

Cold Knap Lake

We once watched a crowd
pull a drowned child from the lake.
Blue-lipped and dressed in water's long green silk
she lay for dead.

Then kneeling on the earth,
a heroine, her red head bowed,
her wartime cotton frock soaked,
my mother gave a stranger's child her breath.
The crowd stood silent,
drawn by the dread of it.

The child breathed, bleating
and rosy in my mother's hands.
My father took her home to a poor house
and watched her thrashed for almost drowning.

Was I there?
Or is that troubled surface something else
shadowy under the dipped fingers of willows
where satiny mud blooms in cloudiness
after the treading, heavy webs of swans
as their wings beat and whistle on the air?

All lost things lie under closing water
in that lake with the poor man's daughter.

Apples

They fill with heat, dewfall, a night of rain.
In a week they have reddened, the seed gone black
in each star-heart. Soft thud of fruit
in the deepening heat of the day.
Out of the delicate petals of secret skin
and that irreversible moment when the fruit set,
such a hard harvest, so cold and sharp on the tongue.

They look up from the grass, too many to save.
A lapful of windfalls with worms in their hearts,
under my thumb the pulse of original sin,
flesh going brown as the skin curls over my knife.
I drown them in water and wine, pushing them under,
then breathe apples simmering in sugar and spice,
fermenting under the tree in sacs of juice
so swollen they'd burst under a wasp's foot.

Oranges

So many of them among the stones,
each like a float over a lobster pot
coming in numerous as the drowned.

Up early at the Little Harbour,
we found the treasure we'd sought
all the Saturdays of childhood.
First gold brought generously
to a mean Britain. I remember
water calm as milk licking
the sand with little oily tongues.

We filled our sleeves,
gathered our skirts to make sacks,
bumped uncomfortably homeward.
Crates like the smashed ribcages of sheep.
Across milky water the wreck
was languorous, her tilted deck
rolling with Atalanta's gold.

Salt at first bite, then bitter pith
and a sharp juice. My tongue searched
for the cloying concentrate I knew
or the scent the miner spoke of,
an orange broken at snap-time underground
breathed a mile away
if the wind's in the right direction.

Talking of Burnings in
Walter Savage Landor's Smithy

The house eases awake to the tick
of clocks, water burbling
in the complexity of drains.
We make slow fires, smoke straight
as a cat's tail against larchwoods.
The Honddu plaits its waters in the rising sun.

Uphill the poet's house lies broken
in a memory of flame.
Face of a stranger in a holy window.
An abbey sacked and word on word
of a monk's patient flamboyance
gilds for a moment and is gone.

Cromwell fires the map.
Peasants come with roaring torches.
A terrorist's bomb.
Another falling wall.
Under the rubble a young girl's voice
blurs to silence as she lets go.

Through house and church and priory
of a tenanted land
the long fires burn, fronds
curling through the heartwood
of great houses, prising stone from stone
in two thousand years of burnings.

With petrol and a match
the ridge-beam goes and the roof sags
like the saddleback of a broken mare.
The displaced leave with their burden,
smoke pressed between scorched sheets,
and all the bridges down.

Marged

I think of her sometimes when I lie in bed,
falling asleep in the room I have made in the roof-space
over the old dark parlŵr where she died
alone in winter, ill and penniless.
Lighting the lamps, November afternoons,
a reading book, whisky gold in my glass.
At my type-writer tapping under stars
at my new roof-window, radio tunes
and dog for company. Or parking the car
where through the mud she called her single cow
up from the field, under the sycamore.
Or looking at the hills she looked at too.
I find her broken crocks, digging her garden.
What else do we share, but being women?

My Box

My box is made of golden oak,
my lover's gift to me.
He fitted hinges and a lock
of brass and a bright key.
He made it out of winter nights,
sanded and oiled and planed,
engraved inside the heavy lid
in brass, a golden tree.

In my box are twelve black books
where I have written down
how we have sanded, oiled and planed,
planted a garden, built a wall,
seen jays and goldcrests, rare red kites,
found the wild heartsease, drilled a well,
harvested apples and words and days
and planted a golden tree.

On an open shelf I keep my box.
Its key is in the lock.
I leave it there for you to read,
or them, when we are dead,
how everything is slowly made,
how slowly things made me,
a tree, a lover, words, a box,
books and a golden tree.

The Hare

i.m. Frances Horovitz 1938–1983

That March night I remember how we heard
a baby crying in a neighbouring room
but found him sleeping quietly in his cot.

The others went to bed and we sat late
talking of children and the men we loved.
You thought you'd like another child. 'Too late.'

you said. And we fell silent, thought a while
of yours with his copper hair and mine,
a grown daughter and sons.

Then, that joke we shared, our phases of the moon.
'Sisterly lunacy' I said. You liked
the phrase. It became ours. Different

as earth and air, yet in one trace that week
we towed the calends like boats reining
the oceans of the world at the full moon.

Suddenly from the fields we heard again
a baby cry, and standing at the door
listened for minutes, eyes and ears soon used

to the night. It was cold. In the east
the river made a breath of shining sound.
The cattle in the field were shadow black.

A cow coughed. Some slept, and some pulled grass.
I could smell blossom from the blackthorn
and see their thorny crowns against the sky.

And then again, a sharp cry from the hill.
'A hare' we said together, not speaking
of fox or trap that held it in a lock

of terrible darkness. Both admitted
next day to lying guilty hours awake
at the crying of the hare. You told me

of sleeping at last in the jaws of a bad dream.
'I saw all the suffering of the world
in a single moment. Then I heard

a voice say "But this is nothing, nothing
to the mental pain".' I couldn't speak of it.
I thought about your dream as you lay ill.

In the last heavy nights before full moon,
when its face seems sorrowful and broken,
I look through binoculars. Its seas flower

like cloud over water, it wears its craters
like silver rings. Even in dying you
menstruated as a woman in health

considering to have a child or no.
When they hand me insults or little hurts
and I'm on fire with my arguments

at your great distance you can calm me still.
Your dream, my sleeplessness, the cattle
asleep under a full moon,

and out there
the dumb and stiffening body of the hare.

February

Lamb-grief in the fields
and a cold as hard as slate.
Foot and hoof are shod

with ice. Our footprints
seem as old as ferns in stone.
Air rings in ash and thorn.

Ice on the rain-butt, thick
as a shield and the tap chokes,
its thumb in its throat.

The stream runs black
in a ruff of ice, its caught breath
furls a frieze of air.

At night ice sings
to the strum of my thrown stones
like a snapped harp-string.

The pond's glass eye holds
leaf, reed, fish, paperweight
in a dream of stone.

Peregrine Falcon

New blood in the killing-ground,
her scullery,
her boneyard.

I touch the raw wire
of vertigo
feet from the edge.

Her house is air. She comes downstairs
on a turn of wind.
This is her table.

She is arrow.
At two miles a minute
the pigeon bursts like a city.

While we turned our backs
she wasted nothing
but a rose-ringed foot

still warm.

Wil Williams (1861–1910)

He kept a garden
like other railwaymen
in that old world of the Great Western.
When his daughter went back
It disappointed her.
How sad, she said,
to see my mother's house so shabby,
the yard-hens scraggy,
the stackyard sour with old hay,
the house dirty.

I can't see the house in her mind,
only the white farm on the hill
that is still there.
Down through the tunnels along the line
they run away from us,
the rooms, the women who tended them,
the dressers of glinting jugs,
the lines of sweet washing between trees.
The stations with their cabbage-patches
and tubbed geraniums are closed
and the trains' long cries are swallowed
in the throats of tunnels.

Annie (1868–1944)

I called her Ga, and a child's stuttered
syllable became her name.
A widow nearly forty years,
beautiful and straight-backed,
always with a bit of lace about her,
pearls the colour of her twisted hair,
the scent of lavender.

It was our job at Fforest to feed the hens
with cool and liquid handfuls of thrown corn.
We looked for eggs smuggled in hedge and hay,
and walked together the narrow path to the sea
calling the seals by their secret names.

At Christmas she rustled packages under her bed
where the po was kept and dusty suitcases.
That year I got an old doll with a china face,
ink-dark eyes and joints at elbows and knees.
Inside her skull, like a tea-pot, under her hair,
beneath her fontanelle, was the cold cave
where her eye-wires rocked her to sleep.

Somewhere in a high hospital window –
I drive past it sometimes with a start of loss –
her pale face made an oval in the glass
over a blue dressing-gown. She waved to me,
too far away to be certain it was her.
They wouldn't let children in.
Then she was lost or somebody gave her away.

The King of Britain's* Daughter

1 Rocking Stone

On the headland is an absence
where it fell some winter night
between here and childhood,
and the sea's still fizzing
over a bruise that will not heal.

A finger would rock it,
Bendigeidfran's stone.
My ear pressed to its flank could hear
the footfall of a storm far out at sea
long before the frown of it darkened the beach.

It purred in wind, was warm against my back
with all the summer in it.
Apple out of legend,
slingstone of Brân's rage against Ireland.
Or so my father said.

2

We'd sing for a bit,
the western sun in our eyes.
Then rocked to sleep in the dark for a hundred miles,

* The giant Bendigeidfran, also known as Brân, son of Llŷr

my face in his coat, soft growl
of the Austin in my dreaming bones,

I'd wake suddenly in a turning lane,
the scut of rabbits in the headlights,
the glint of two churns on the stand,
a rutted track over fields,
two gates that had to be opened and closed again.

Then the deep cloud-cold of a feather bed,
mirrors that bloomed with a damp off the sea,
and under the oak bed in the black cave
where the ghost was, and a fleece of dust,
the po, with its garland of roses.

3

Above the house a cat's-tail rises from the fire
his mother lit a generation back.
Beneath her plum-trees air takes up the slack
in someone else's sheets. At dusk

she'll gather their cloudiness off the evening sea,
indoors, cast one and watch it settle
for the keel of her iron to plough,
her glasses misting in a hiss of starch.

5

His hat covered my eyes
and his coat dragged in the grass,
the pockets too deep to fathom.

When she gave it away

– it was old, the tweed threadbare,
the gold words faded like old books
inside the headband –

she gave away mornings of forage,
beachcombings, blackberries, pebbles, eggs,
field-mushrooms with pleated linings,

his fist working it to a form
for the leveret that quivered under my hand
before it died.

6

When the world wobbled
we heard it on a radio chained
by its fraying plait of wires
to the kitchen window-sill
between a sheaf of letters,
bills and things needing to be done,
and a jar of marigolds.

And over its Bakelite crown
the sea, level as milk.
The news came out of the sky,
a mist off the sea,
an incoming shadow
of rain or wings.

7

Gorse, knowing no season
of war or winter or times
not flowering, not kissing,
was always yellow,
a burning bush all summer,
but in winter just
one unblinking eye,
a small flame dreaming in a bush
before they fired it,
and the whole cliff burned.

14

Wind's in the limekilns, hollow-eyed,
blind with nettles and pebbles.
Above the spilt light of the stream
the houseboat lolled in the stones,
horizon askew. Spiders wove their latitudes
and longitudes across the porthole.

Day after day we put to sea on a drift of sand,
baling rain from the hull with a tin can,
the hold full of pebbles, oranges,
a glass-stoppered bottle of dandelion burdock,
the *Beano* for the long hours on watch,
the bathers my mother knitted from unpicked cardigans.

Always the skew horizon, and a cave-breath
of salt and fish and rot that I still catch
with a shiver of pleasure.
Day after day we sailed the weather west,
dreaming of Bendigeidfran
towing his rage through the sea.

There's not a plank left,
but round the headland where the stone fell,
black rocks shelve, and the rising tide
drowns the print where his great foot stamped.
In a slither of muscle and fins, the grey Atlantic
settles to green in the arms of the bay.

Today I swim beyond the empty headland
in search of the giant's stone.
Do I see it through green translucent water,
shadow of a wreck, a drowned man's shoulder,
a clavicle huge as a ship's keel
wedged between rocks?

Radio Engineer

i The Heaviside Layer

Staring into the starry sky, that time
in the darkest dark of war and countryside,
'What is the stars?'
my father asked,

then told me that up there,
somewhere between us and Orion,
hangs the ionosphere, lower, closer at night,
reflecting his long wave signals back to earth,

light bending in water.
But things get tight and close,
words, music, languages
all breathing together under that old *carthen*,

Cardiff, Athlone, Paris
all tongue-twisted up,
all crackle and interference,
your ears hearing shimmer

like trying to stare at stars.

iii

With wires, transmitters, microphones,
my father unreeled his line

to cast his singing syllables at the sky,
unleashed and riding airwaves up and up

to touch and be deflected,
moths at a silver window in the air.

I saw it, a cast line falling back
through shaken light above the pool,

sound parting water
like a hare in corn.

iv

Outside in the graveyard
I collected frozen roses,
an alabaster dove with a broken wing
for my hoard in the long grass,

while he unreeled his wires down the aisle,
hitched a microphone to the pulpit
and measured silence with a quick chorus
from the *Messiah*.

Still I can't look at stars,
or lean with a telescope, dizzy, against the turning earth,
without asking again, 'What is the stars?'
or calling 'Testing, testing' into the dark.

Musician

for Owain

His carpet splattered like a Jackson Pollock
with clothes, books, instruments, the *NME*,
he strummed all day, read Beethoven sonatas.
He could hear it, he said, 'like words.'

That bitterest winter, he took up the piano, obsessed,
playing Bartok in the early hours. Snow fell,
veil after veil till we lost the car in the drive.
I slept under two duvets and my grandmother's fur,
and woke, suffocating, in the luminous nights
to hear the Hungarian Dances across moonlit snow.
The street cut off, immaculate, the house
glacial, suburbs hushed in wafery whiteness.
At dawn, hearing Debussy, I'd find him,
hands in fingerless gloves against the cold,
overcoat on. He hadn't been to bed.

Snows banked the doors, rose to the sills,
silted the attic, drew veils across the windows.
Scent, sound, colour, detritus lay buried.
I dreamed the house vaulted and pillared with snow,
a drowned cathedral, waiting for the thaw,
and woke to hear the piano's muffled bells,
a first pianissimo slip of snow from the roof.

Anorexic

My father's sister,
the one who died
before there was a word for it,
was fussy with her food.
'Eat up,' they'd say to me,
ladling a bowl with warning.

What I remember's
how she'd send me to the dairy,
taught me to take cream,
the standing gold.
Where the jug dipped
I saw its blue-milk skin
before the surface healed.

Breath held, tongue between teeth,
I carried in the cream,
brimmed, level,
parallel, I knew,
with that other, hidden horizon
of the earth's deep
ungleaming water-table.

And she, more often than not half-dressed,
stockings, a slip, a Chinese kimono,
would warm the cream, pour it
with crumbled melting cheese
over a delicate white cauliflower,
or field mushrooms
steaming in porcelain,

then watch us eat, relishing,
smoking her umpteenth cigarette,
glamorous, perfumed, starved,
and going to die.

The Vet

'Would the child like to leave?
It won't be pleasant.'

But I'm stuck with it,
brazening out the cowshed
and the chance of horror,
not knowing how to leave
once I'd said I'd stay.

Gloved to the elbow in blood
and her mysterious collar of muscle,
he wrenched from the deep cathedral of her belly
where her heart hung and the calf swam in its pool,
a long bellowing howl
and a rope of water.

I got off lightly that time,
no knife, no severing,
no inter-uterine butchery
to cut them free.

He let go the rope of water
and the calf swam home like a salmon
furled in a waterfall,
gleaming, silver, sweet under the tongue
of his brimming mother.

Lament

For the green turtle with her pulsing burden,
in search of the breeding-ground.
For her eggs laid in their nest of sickness.

For the cormorant in his funeral silk,
the veil of iridescence on the sand,
the shadow on the sea.

For the ocean's lap with its mortal stain.
For Ahmed at the closed border.
For the soldier in his uniform of fire.

For the gunsmith and the armourer,
the boy fusilier who joined for the company,
the farmer's sons, in it for the music.

For the hook-beaked turtles,
the dugong and the dolphin,
the whale struck dumb by the missile's thunder.

For the tern, the gull and the restless wader,
the long migrations and the slow dying,
the veiled sun and the stink of anger.

For the burnt earth and the sun put out,
the scalded ocean and the blazing well.
For vengeance, and the ashes of language.

The Field-Mouse

Summer, and the long grass is a snare drum,
The air hums with jets.
Down at the end of the meadow,
far from the radio's terrible news,
we cut the hay. All afternoon
its wave breaks before the tractor blade.
Over the hedge our neighbour travels his field
in a cloud of lime, drifting our land
with a chance gift of sweetness.

The child comes running through the killed flowers,
his hands a nest of quivering mouse,
its black eyes two sparks burning.
We know it'll die, and ought to finish it off.
It curls in agony big as itself
and the star goes out in its eye.
Summer in Europe, the fields hurt,
and the children kneel in long grass
staring at what we have crushed.

Before day's done the field lies bleeding,
the dusk garden inhabited by the saved, voles,
frogs, a nest of mice. The wrong that woke
from a rumour of pain won't heal,
and we can't face the newspapers.
All night I dream the children dance in grass,
their bones brittle as mouse-ribs, the air
stammering with gunfire, my neighbour turned
stranger, wounding my land with stones.

Ark

'Keeping the seed alive upon the face of
all the earth once the fountains of the deep
and the windows of the sky are stopped.'
                                    — Genesis

1

Winter of rain, the rivers of Europe too big for themselves,
and the oceans rising. The sea's at the door. It curls into the cellar,
climbs the stairs, laps the threshold of cities.
Coastal towns go under. A church falls to the waves.
Only the watchman awake to cry 'flood' in the drunken palace
as the wall is breached and the sea takes Cantre'r Gwaelod.
Only a boy with his thumb in the dyke as the low countries drown.

2

From Oxfam, an ark of gopher wood,
each beast so crude I can't name it for sure:
elephant, tiger, zebra, two maned lions, no lioness,
white creatures tall as camels or giraffes.
Could they be sheep?

3

Rain falls through February, March.
'Of every clean beast thou shall take to thee by sevens.'
Beulah Speckle-faced, and three black faced ewes.
The flock puddles the field to mud.
We wake nightly in the early hours, dress for the rain,
to count their faces in the flashlight, their glittering eyes.

A sudden day of light and the March wind's home
like a hare running. The flock is moonlit cloud,
their breath starlight. One ewe stands alone
turning and turning, pawing the ground.
The horizons in the gold-green of her eyes
know the midwife in me before I do.

You hold her shoulders and talk tenderly.
The scalding cave's familiar as soapy washing,
in my hand a sodden head, the slippery pebbles
of hooves. Out of the bone ark adrift
on its flood I bring the lamb. Its skull
is the moon on my palm,

the four of us murmuring, earthed again,
getting our bearings.

A Difficult Birth, Easter 1998

An old ewe that somehow till this year
had given the ram the slip. We thought her barren.
Good Friday, and the Irish peace deal close,
and tonight she's serious, restless and hoofing the straw.
We put off the quiet supper and bottle of wine
we'd planned, to celebrate if the news is good.

Her waters broke an hour ago and she's sipped
her own lost salty ocean from the ground.
While they slog it out in Belfast, eight decades
since Easter 1916, exhausted, tamed by pain,
she licks my fingers with a burning tongue,
lies down again. Two hooves and a muzzle.

But the lamb won't come. You phone for help
and step into the lane to watch for car lights.
This is when the whitecoats come to the women,
well-meaning, knowing best, with their needles and forceps.
So I ease my fingers in, take the slippery head
in my right hand, two hooves in my left.

We strain together, harder than we dared.
I feel a creak in the limbs and pull till he comes
in a syrupy flood. She drinks him, famished, and you find us
peaceful, at a cradling that might have been a death.
Then the second lamb slips through her opened door,
the stone rolled away.

Architect

When he sets his board in the long grass of Perigord
in the ellipse he mowed under the *Prunus niger*,
as to the one star of a house on the mountain,
all earth's lines come running to him:

Gossamers, corn-drills, bean-rows, Roman roads and passes,
poplars lined-up all ways over deep grasses,
massive limestone in the mason's yard,
rusting steel girders, sawn timber, scented wood,

a tractor mumbling down hill, deliberate,
slow and measured, trying to get things straight
all the hay-making afternoon, overhead
the swallows' tangled airy latitudes.

All day, a 3H pencil on its compass turning
and weighed with its own shadow, the red tree burning.

Glass

Her Table

She fussed between kitchen and dining room
giving us all things to carry and do.
I see her two hands polishing a wine glass
until it gleams, immaculate.
She lifts it to the light and sets it down
on starched damask on the Christmas table.

On an ordinary Sunday it would be
a cut-glass jug of water, four tumblers.
As if these things could hold us, as if
they could make us flawless and ring true.

The Habit Of Light

In the early evening, she liked to switch on the lamps
in corners, on low tables, to show off her brass,
her polished furniture, her silver and glass.
At dawn she'd draw all the curtains back for a glimpse
of the cloud-lit sea. Her oak floors flickered
in an opulence of beeswax and light.
In the kitchen, saucepans danced their lids, the kettle purred
on the Aga, supper on its breath and the buttery melt
of a pie, and beyond the swimming glass of old windows,
in the deep perspective of the garden, a blackbird singing,

she'd come through the bean rows in tottering shoes,
her pinny full of strawberries, a lettuce, bringing
the palest potatoes in a colander, her red hair bright
with her habit of colour, her habit of light.

Migraine

Here it comes again: vision bevel-edged
with rainbows, stuff dissolving even as I look
to liquid light, the firm world swimming
just beyond the rim of things.

There's a remedy today: the *migraleve*
they gave me from her medicine cupboard,
I being the daughter who'd inherited this,
and her skin, and the early grey in our hair.

It's the last thing I should be doing,
squinting at a screen at the still centre,
getting the words down before the onset
of vertigo and steel drums.

Then all I'll want is the green curtains drawn
in her room in the afternoon, sun-arrows splintering
her dressing table to a clutter of brushes and combs,
dustings of powder, its lipsticks and eau de cologne.

And her duck-down pillows and old-rose eiderdown,
her hand weightless and cool on my brow,
changing the scalding flannel for the cold one.
'A sick headache', they called it, when I was an infant.

She taught me to lie so still, the pain wouldn't find me.
If I drifted to sleep, she would creep away,
lifting her cool hand
too lightly to wake me.

The Croquet Set

A box of varnished wood,
frayed rope handles at each end.
Every year on the first day of summer
he'd ease the creak from the hinges
with a trace of green, iridescent oil.

Eight worn mallets, their shafts warped,
blue, yellow, purple. Mine was the red one.
The brown one nobody wanted. Hoops, posts,
eight wooden balls, all colour
knocked out of them, and the rules lost.

No rush. No slapdash setting out.
She stepped into the garden with a tinkling tray
as he mowed the lawn to stripes, unruled his tape
over the grass. The knock of wood on wood,
our shadows so long we were taller than trees.

The man takes cash, knocks fifteen pounds off.
This one's from a French château,
but under the lid it's all mine now
and I take back from the dark one hour so bright
there seemed an even chance of getting it right.

Quince

I planted a quince for her, completing the ellipse
of fruiting trees – plum, apple, an apricot
grown from a stone – for its colour and grace.
But six weeks after her death, it's not the bitterness
of quince that has me by the throat again,
but the *acer* tossing its red hair
under the running skies of May,
the tree whose leaves she untangled
with hands that untangled my hair.

Amber

Coveted week after week on the market stall,
coiled, nonchalant, arrayed under the lid
of locked glass, they grew familiar.
She'd finger them, drop them over her head,
try them for size, spoilt for choice –
red-amber, yellow, cut Russian ruby,
or those sad rosaries, widow's beads of Whitby jet.
In each bead surfaced the cloudy face of a woman.

Warmed by the sunlight on dressing tables,
or against a woman's skin, then laid safe
in a drawer each night between the silk leaves
of her underwear. Never cold, as if
each bead were an unquenchable flame
that burned a million years like a sanctuary lamp
beneath the ice, each drip of sticky gold
hardening to honeyed stone.

As if nothing that has ever contained heat
can be cold again, mirrors never empty
and our rooms, furniture, hoarded amulets,
could reassemble themselves into a life
and still pass hand to hand from underneath
the permafrost, ice woman to living daughter.

The White Ship

On the kitchen table he made me a ship –
war on the wave-lengths,
Children's Hour, tea,
and the roads locked in snow.

The News was dark with sinkings,
shadows in the sea, talk of U-boats,
sinister submarine things
that could tow you down.

What signal calls it back now?
The hull in his hands,
bone-webbed, fingerprinted
among slivers of wood and glue.

We came home from the beach,
with a wreckage of leavings –
oiled ropes, driftwood,
a crate of oranges.

So he built my boat
from a baulk of ship's timber
thrown up in a storm
from the war-wounded sea.

He worked all that winter,
set a radio in the engine-room,
then painted her white
as the ship on every horizon.

One Sunday in spring
we launched her on the lake.
'*The Queen Mary*,' he said
as she slipped his hands.

She set off for perilous waters
in a scatter of swans and marvelling boys,
dancing to port and starboard,
till her course set westwards

at the star of my will. And the radio
calls her back from the deep.

The Lace-Maker

A white farm, a black beach
and the long seas running.
At the click of the gate three gulls lift
from the sea and the wind sucks salt, fish
and cat-piss from the old lime-kilns.

She comes between trees to fetch me home,
her apron full of pegs, her lace
cuffing the stones below the waterfall,
pearls beading the air, and in each hand
is one warm egg, laid wild.

Her sheets are out above the field,
tugging for Ireland in a westerly,
billowing slips for pillows and bolsters,
table cloths, petticoats,
angels in lace and clean linen.

She calls, shading her eyes from too much
sea-light, from straining too long, too often
by the wavering light of oil-lamps,
gas-light, a primitive electricity
too frail to stand those wild Atlantic winters,

when at the table she counted her stitches home
in a system of bobbins and beads till every tea
and bed-time were washed in the settled foam
of sea-flowers hooked in a detritus of bird-bones,
her knuckles ivoried with listening.

Women's Work

Their books come with me, women writers,
their verses borne through the rooms
out between the plum trees to the field,
as an animal will gather things,
a brush, a bone, a shoe,
for comfort against darkness.

August Sunday morning,
and I'm casting for words,
wandering the garden sipping their poems,
leaving cups of them here and there in the grass
where the washing steams in the silence
after the hay-days and the birdsong months.

I am sixteen again, and it's summer,
and the sisters are singing, their habits gathered,
sleeves rolled for kitchen work,
rosy hands hoisting cauldrons of greens.
The laundry hisses with steam-irons
glossing the collars of our summer blouses.

Then quietly they go along white gravel,
telling their beads in the walled garden
where *Albertine*'s heady rosaries spill
religious and erotic over the hot stones.
And there's restlessness in the summer air,
like this desire for poems,

our daily offices.

Snow

The dreamed Christmas,
flakes shaken out of silences so far
and starry we can't sleep for listening
for papery rustles out there in the night
and wake to find our ceiling glimmering,
the day a psaltery of light.

So we're out over the snow fields
before it's all seen off with a salt-lick
of Atlantic air, then home at dusk, snow-blind
from following chains of fox and crow and hare,
to a fire, a roasting bird, a ringing phone,
and voices wondering where we are.

A day foretold by images
of glassy pond, peasant and snowy roof
over the holy child iconed in gold.
Or women shawled against the goosedown air
pleading with soldiers at a shifting frontier
in the snows of television,

while in the secret dark a fresh snow falls
filling our tracks with stars.

Into the Mountain

after slate sculpture by Howard Bowcott

1

Sedimentary silt's
slow metamorphosis,
mudstone to shale,
then the squeeze
of the giant's fist.

Light fingers it
with a shimmer like water
on roofscape or slate tip.
A rockface flickers in the wind
as if it moved.

2

Slate to sleep under,
knowing its rain-blue gleam
or the satin of moonlight.
To walk on, cool underfoot,
carrying a tray into the garden

where once Nain stumped in her clogs,
goosefeathers drifting the flags,
and her bucket of water
flung on the dairy floor
ran the gutters blue with milk.

Slabs to set jellies,
cool curds and junkets,
butter slapped to a pattern of oak leaves,
a cheese to be turned,
a beaded jug of milk.

3

His lungs filled
with sediment,
invisible blues, purples,
silty darknesses.
Their branches brimmed
with a shadow of stone
till he couldn't walk, or breathe.
They offered him
a settlement of dust.

4

So slow the strata,
fossils and globules of oil
trapped between pages,
the laying down
of the leaves of slate.

Now, inside mountains,
in the cathedrals of silence,
streams break their beads
into the dark, a fall of vertebrae
too far down to hear.

It begins again,
a fall of earth.
Between history's pages
they will find the body of a man
like a fern.

The Paddle Steamers

In the great grey tank of the rising sea
muscular river and sea-currents flex
and the Severn's wrestle of waters
cracks two shores open.

Dawn a quiver on a bedroom ceiling
and it's quick, up and away,
with bread and cheese, windfalls
and dandelion burdock,
the flash of clean white daps on the pedals.

Drop a bike on the stones,
step under the echoing cold of the pier,
pick lapis blue mussels and amberweed necklaces
from the terrible stanchions of rust,
wait for the paddle steamer rounding the headland.

Sometimes it was me in the prow
of *Glen Usk, Ravenswood, The Cardiff Queen,*
waves oiling apart to port and starboard,
light a slither of water-snakes,
a whiplash of metals and mermaid hair.

The tide recedes, taking its time.
Away it slides over the mud-flats
leaving a gleam of pebbles, crustacea, driftwood,
and a rusty bicycle without wheels.

Voicing The Organ

He must voice the organ. Twenty two tons of machine
must be taught to whisper like teaching a glacier to thaw.
Over the sea from Aabenraa, each pipe
hand-planed and sanded to silk, swell-boxes, windchests
of pine, their secret interiors stroked like skin.
Hand-carved rods. Oak and cherry, rosewood,
mahogany, walnut, ebony, each in its place.
Four winter months he works with thousands of pieces
like the puzzle of bones of a whale from the permafrost
that has forgotten its song.

He voices the whale, works in the silent nights,
the auditorium deaf to the cries of the city.
He listens, head cocked as the thrush on the lawn, his touch
so light, stroking and easing, till all pipes in a rank,
all notes in a stop sing with the same timbre,
all seventy-six stops with their beautiful names,
Principal, Octave, Quint and Cornet,
Voix Celeste, Voix Humaine, celestial and human,
a perfect choir, as if voicing the organ had given it a soul.

For the first time after the ice, the high notes,
first drops out of silence, then the beginning
of trickling, the beginning of streams, rivers,
then thundering torrents and the wind roaring over the ice.
And with the thaw the pain must begin,
the cry of an earth that's alive again.

As they switch on the lights in the steel web of the ceiling,
five thousand pipes will gleam in a breaking wave
of steel. The audience will come, taking their places
with a collective murmur of pleasure, the house lights dim,
the organist arrive, the first notes sound in the hush.
And the anonymous man who listened late
into winter nights for the accent of every stop,
who voiced it in the silence of the night,
will be somewhere else, letting it go.

Sloes

The year he died, never so many mushrooms,
and sloes blue in their crowns of thorns.
Day after day we were out gathering,
cramming jars, stowing the freezer,

till the house was a spice-box of eastern names,
ginger, cinnamon, vanilla, star anise,
in their aromatic syrups. Baskets
filled with fungi, plushy, pink-gilled,

too many to eat, lifted from the morning
grass, warm as new eggs.
The best steamed in butter. The rest
darkened in the fridge to a musky rot.

The children picked the sloes, out
so long I stood, uneasy,
folding clothes from the line,
calling their names over the fields.

They ran up the lane with their jewels,
their hands and faces stained with juice,
the enamel-blue bloom of the thorn-fruit
blackening with their finger prints.

Months passed him by, his gold ring
loosening on his finger. That winter,
when the gin was dark as blood
and turned us tipsy, he had gone.

We kept one bottle longer than the rest,
forgot it in the back of the cupboard,
and found it, tidying up, uncorked it,
and wondered at the taste of shadows in it.

Translation

after translating from Welsh,
particularly a novel by Kate Roberts

Your hand on her hand – you've never been
this close to a woman since your mother's beauty
at the school gate took your breath away,
since you held hot sticky hands with your best friend,
since you, schoolgirl guest in a miner's house,
two up, two down, too small for guest rooms
or guest beds, shared with two sisters,
giggling in the dark, hearts hot with boy-talk.

You spread the script. She hands you a fruit.
You break it, eat, know exactly how
to hold its velvet weight, to bite, to taste it
to the last gold shred. But you're lost for words,
can't think of the English for *eirin* – it's on the tip of your –
But the cat ate your tongue, licking peach juice
from your palm with its rough *langue de chat*,
tafod cath, the rasp of loss.

In the Beginning

'on her 7th birthday'

Holy Bible – the King James version,
soft black leather cover,
tissue pages edged in gold.
I loved the maps, the names: Jerusalem.
Askelon. The Wilderness of Shur.

And the old photographs:
caught by a camera in black and white,
women drawing water at a well,
a fisherman on the Sea of Galilee
blurred people scything corn,
mountains sharp, stone still forever.

I see it all in colour, a girl my age
two thousand years ago, or sixty years,
or now in a desert land at war, squatting
among the sheaves, arms raised,
threshing grain with a flail.

Threshing with a flail. That's it. Words
from another language, a narrative of spells
in difficult columns on those moth-thin pages,
words to thrill the heart with a strange music,
words like flail, and wilderness,
and in the beginning.

Mother Tongue

You'd hardly call it a nest,
just a scrape in the stones,
but she's all of a dither
warning the wind and sky
with her desperate cries.

If we walk away
she'll come home quiet
to the warm brown pebble
with its cargo of blood and hunger,
where the future believes in itself,

and the beat of the sea
is the pulse of a blind
helmeted embryo afloat
in the twilight of the egg,
learning the language.

The Fisherman

for Ted Hughes

From his pool of light in the crowded room, alone,
the poet reads to us. The sun slinks off
over darkening fields, and the moon is a stone
rolled and tumbled in the river's grief.

In a revolving stillness at the edge
of turbulent waters, the salmon hangs its ghost
in amber. On the shore of the white page
the fisherman waits. His line is cast.

The house is quiet. Under its thatch
it is used to listening. It's all ears
for the singing line out-reeled from his touch
till the word rises with its fin of fire.

The tremor in the voice betrays a hand
held tense above the surface of that river,
patient at the deep waters of the mind
for a haul of dangerous silver,

till electricity's earthed, and hand on heart
the line that arcs from air to shore is art.

The Piano

The last bus sighs through the stops of the sleeping suburb
and he's home again with a click of keys, a step on the stairs.
I see him again, shut in the upstairs sitting-room
in that huge Oxfam overcoat, one hand shuffling
through the music, the other lifting the black wing.

My light's out in the room he was born in. In the hall
the clock clears its throat and counts twelve hours
into space. His scales rise, falter and fall back –
not easy to fly on one wing, even for him
with those two extra digits he was born with.

I should have known there'd be music as he flew, singing,
and the midwife cried out, 'Magic fingers!' A small variation,
born with more, like obsession. They soon fell,
tied like the cord, leaving a small scar fading
on each hand like a memory of flight.

Midnight arpeggios, Bartok, Schubert. I remember,
kept in after school, the lonely sound of a piano lesson
through an open window between-times, sun on the lawn
and everyone gone, the piece played over and over
to the metronome of tennis. Sometimes in the small hours,

after two, the hour of his birth, I lose myself listening
to that little piece by Schubert, perfected in the darkness
of space where the stars are so bright they cast shadows,
and I wait for that waterfall of notes, as if
two hands were not enough.

Erik Satie and the Blackbird

on listening to Satie's 'Vexations' played
from noon to dawn by a relay of pianists
in Salem Chapel, Hay-on-Wye

The blackbird sings
for eighteen hours
with a bead of rain
in its throat.
First notes at first light.
Four in the morning
and he'll be there
with his mouth full of gold.

The piano crosses an ocean
on one wing,
noon to midnight
and through to dawn.
This is the nightshift.
you and the rain
and the pianist awake,
navigating the small hours.

While the blackbird sleeps
under a dark wing,
the town breathing,
the wash of a car on a wet street,

the world turns over
in the dark. The sleepless
travel on. They know by heart
their own refrains.

The pianist doesn't turn the page.
Just back to the top
where music collects
opening its throat to the rain,
and somewhere two bells
count down the hours
towards first light, landfall,
the downpour of a blackbird singing.

RS

for the poet R. S. Thomas, 1913–2000

His death
on the midnight news.
Suddenly colder.

Gold September's driven off
by something afoot
in the south-west approaches.

God's breathing in space out there
misting the heave of the seas
dark and empty tonight,

except for the one frail coracle
borne out to sea,
burning.

The Stone Poems

Rock

In the subdivisions of geological time
Earth story's chaptered with eras,
paragraphed with epochs, ages, chrons,
sedimentary time laid down and shaped
with the patience of stone, silt on silt,
microbe, algae, trilobite, brachiopod,
first jellyfish, first worm,
leaf-mould, bone on bone.
Then the long upheavals, continents
lapping like plates of a baby's skull.

Hay

Speaking of stone on a day like this,
the silence, the heat, the hay-days,
when the slates creak in the sun,
the flags are too hot for the dog
and the field's dried to a thin song
of seeds and grasshoppers,
yellow rattle, harebells, the litany of grass,

any moment now there'll be the growl
of a neighbour's tractor on the lane,
then the swishing scissors of the mowing machine,

and every last grass and fallen flower of the field
by nightfall cooling under the moon
is dependent on neighbourhood
and the nourishment of rock.

Granite

Vertiginous numbers:
seven-hundred million years,
granite from Pembrokeshire. Is it this
we tread on, this starry pavement,
the Milky Way underfoot?

Go sandalled over pavements set with granite
in a southern city of squares and geraniums,
alleyways cats-cradled with ellipses,
laundry blown in a warm wind
and bed linen laid to air over granite sills.

Sit at a cafe table in the dusk,
a glass of wine, a floor hewn from the batholith.
Take a loosened piece in your hand,
a paving sett to turn under the light
so small and heavy it can teach you gravity.

Slate

It arrived from Gwynedd, Penrhyn slate
palletted, piled on the drive,
settled from silts and mudstones
five hundred and twenty million years ago,
bruised purple by so much time,
a history book, its pages open
for the text of lichens and weather.

It roofed Europe, made floors so cold
the rheum seeped through their bones.
Hearthstone. Threshold. Gate-post.
Dairy slabs where cream was rising gold,
and butter came in the churn, patted and ridged
with a wooden spade carved with a sheaf of wheat,
salt-butter left on a slate to bead
between the bivalves of two plates.

Like this old house between the saucers
of floor and roof, a pigeon's throat
of lapping purples, lilacs, greys,
feathering our nest under the stars.

Edward Llwyd and the Trilobite

ORDOVICIAN

Edward Llwyd, he was the curious one,
the Snowdon Lily already to his name,
nose down among the very stones of the earth,
noting 'divers flatfish' in the rocks.

Llandeilo, sixteen-ninety-nine. Forget
all that we know. Un-name the stones, the fossils,
untell the age of the Ordovician.
Count biblical time from the seventh day.

Their world was created in four-thousand-and-four BC,
and the stone fish he netted from Carmarthen silts
were 'figured stones' placed there by God, creation's
little finishing touches, like the stars in heaven.

A strike of his hammer broke the heart of limestone
clean as a conker, and a trilobite stared
with four-hundred and sixty-five-million-year-old eyes
from a dark age deeper than his fathoming.

Landfall

Wake in a blaze of moonlight.
Sit up too quickly. Dizzy. Don't
be surprised to find yourself in the Silurian,
your house in deep water.

On the map of the past
this place was far out at sea,
old Ceredigion not born
from the Iapetus Ocean.

Land out of its depth, finding fall
from Aberystwyth grits and mudstones,
storm-driven sands out of waters
too old and too deep for life.

So your bed's on the tilt and spinning,
walls cart-wheeling on four corners,
then the oak chest slides, sucked down
the turbidity currents of sleep.

Your body knows this.
Walk the cliffs. Look down
to a tumble of choughs, and farther, below,
a sea-locked cove of ochre sand you yearn for.

Feel vertigo's pendulum pull at your heart,
and underground, underfoot,
the powerful surge of the Iapetus Ocean
dragging its tether.

Woman Washing her Hair

DEVONIAN

for David

A block of yellow sandstone in the sun.
You tap and chisel in the open air
until you find her in the coarse-grain stone,
a woman on her haunches, pouring her hair.

Curled, primitive, crouched on the folds
of her thighs. You comb stone into strands
furrowed like the steep fields
of Brecon's old red ploughland,

like plaiting and contending waterfalls,
sands and sediments, the dreadlocks of the sea.
Half emerged, unfinished, not quite free,
slowly the sandstone woman, leaning still

over waters that are not quite there,
crouches, washing her hair.

The Stone Hare

LOWER CARBONIFEROUS

for Meic Watts

Think of it waiting three hundred million years,
not a hare hiding in the last stand of wheat,
but a premonition of stone, a moonlit reef
where corals reached for the light through clear
waters of warm Palaeozoic seas.
In its limbs lies the story of the earth,
the living ocean, then the slow birth
of limestone from the long trajectories
of starfish, feather-stars, crinoids and crushed shells
that fill with calcite, harden, wait for the quarryman,
the timed explosion and the sculptor's hand.
Then the hare, its eye a planet, springs from the chisel
to stand in the grass, moonlight's muscle and bone,
the stems of sea lilies slowly turned to stone.

Coal

UPPER CARBONIFEROUS

for Glyndŵr Thomas, 1915–1995

From Abercarn, Gwent,
from the tropical swamp that laid down the coal

he cut when he was a boy,
fourteen years old and a real man now,
working the stint at his father's side,

Deep under the earth, labouring at the face
in lamp-swept darkness, he'd ache
at a sudden breath of bluebells brought
by a May wind in the downdraft,
for the sunlit woods he'd miss that shift.

We bring in a scuttleful, every shovel
haunted by hands, hibernating newts,
little dragons of damp places,
saved one by one from the fire,
their fingers cold on our skin.

Mesozoic

Time of the dinosaur.
First paw-print. First hoofbeat.
First mammals of swamp and shore,
first of the cold-bloods dreaming on stones.

And at its humid, balmy close,
ammonite and dinosaur dead,
rich silts flood the valleys,
and the garden begins.

Nine Green Gardens

At Aberglasne

'He has a proud hall.
A fortress made bright by whitewash
And encompassing it all around,
Nine green gardens.'
  – Lewys Glyn Cothi (c. 1420–1489)

The Yew Tunnel in Winter

Listen to sap rise, unstoppable flood,
for all the centuries as the tap-roots grew,
pumping through branches to the stirring bud
from deepest earth. In graveyards they say a yew
sends a root into the mouths of all the dead.
Here, sense all that power snowed in and still,
shut in the dream of winter and history
at the end of a muffled lane below Grongar Hill.
The garden's under wraps. The sorrow trees
let in, like moonlight, little webs of snow,
white footfalls through the arching clerestories.
Grown from a seed five centuries ago
from the gut of a bird, the Age of Hywel done,
the poetry of gardens yet to come.

The Parapet Walk

Rumours of religious settlements
leave silences among the cloister stones,
and underfoot, a shadow in each cowled arch.
Cron Gaer. A circle hill-fort. Roman and Celt.
The Kingdom of Hywel Dda. Even their bones
are gone, ground to a fine tilth under mulch,
leaf-mould, soils and river-silts.
Lewys Glyn Cothi's nine green gardens
folded in fields of war named bloodily
like our century's fields of guilt,
Cae Tranc, Cae Dial, Cae'r Ochain, Cadfan.
The words are blood and bone of butchery.
Whitsun, 1257, the battle of Coed Llathen,
a thousand Saxons dead, brief victory Llywelyn's.

The Cloister Garden

When he came home to Aberglasne,
crusader, troubadour, on the road from Europe,
shouldering arms, a lute, a sack of dreams,
did he, poet or soldier, bring from Italy
a vision of a garden on a slope
above a valley fed with mountain streams?
Abbot. Landowner. Who planned
this cloister garden apt to the inclination
of the hill? Who set a pavement here
for gentry to stroll on levelled land

or a ghost to go in slippered contemplation
under the ancient shadow of Cron Gaer?
Either way, it's here, the hanging garden
of another time, a rediscovered Eden.

A Sad Story

Places are made of hearsay and story.
There's talk in these trees of five young servant girls
found dead in their beds one winter morning,
choked, they say, by the fumes of a blocked chimney.
That dawn the house woke to cold ash, no curl
of smoke from thirty hearths burning.
The silence of the dead instead of chatter
and quick feet running on the stairs,
fuel for the fires and jugs of scalding water,
slop buckets, sculleries awash, clatter
of crockery on slate, the chink of silver.
People of no account, poor farmers' daughters.
No names. No documents. No graves. Instead
just talk of a tragedy, five young girls dead.

Church Wood

Beyond the wall and the ruined aviary,
a wood where trees shadow a small pool.
Outside the wire the fields are nitrogen green.
Away from the house and its raucous rookery,

the contemplation garden's quiet and cool.
We walk as if we own the place, unseen
in the privacy and silence of still water.
Somewhere, the gunfire of a wren in an ash.
To the north, the Via Julia Maritima,
now become the humming loud A40.
John Dyer's Grongar Hill lies west
beyond the garden's *terza rima*.
A poet shares a gardener's grand design:
sound, pattern, meaning, double digging, line.

The Upper Walled Garden

In the hot box of the upper walled garden
raised beds lie ready for the gardener's design,
a Celtic cross, two circles cut by paths,
a red kite's view of curve and line.
Aconitum, Alchemilla, Amaryllis, Angelica

Down here in the heat, two survivors: a fig tree
rooted in the wall, and an ancient apple leans
its weight against the earth, its hard fruit set
among the drum and dither of wild bees.
Camassia, Campanula, Clematis, Crocosmia

Once a kitchen garden, hives under apple trees,
where maids came gathering for the table.
A litany of plant names now, and earthy airs
rise from the garden's seething crucible.
Euphorbia, Rudbeckia, Iris germanica.

Listen to the garden's Latin, the *missa cantata*
Of *Wisteria sinensis, Prunus lusitanica.*

The Lower Walled Garden

Past the old apple tree askew the path,
down through the door in the wall. A blackbird singing.
Young sapling trees still potted and bound.
Malus sargentii, browned in the aftermath
of a late frost. Silvers of a buzzard turning.
It could be the secret garden, the one not found,
garden beyond garden deep in the lee
of Grongar hill. From the sky you'd see a view
of four rectangles edged with box,
a tunnel of crab apple trees
and future walks in shady avenues
on crossed paths with a roundel at the crux,
and off centre, at the heart, an apple tree,
its fallen shadow old as history.

The Pool Garden

The cuckoo's late, two notes in the weeping ash.
Last call, C and A flat, before
its voice breaks and the summer's older.
The kite circles land grown lush
with sorrows of another century's war.

In garlands of builder's ribbon, gaudy
oceans of crumpled plastic, a machine
leans on its claw. The clay is caterpillar
tracked with chevrons, the water cloudy
from the digger's delicate bucket work, green
with weed and reflections. Once viticulture
flourished where the hot border's planned
on the south wall. A thrush picks the churned soil,
alone with the garden gods beside the pool.

The Stream Garden

Damp ground between the pool garden and the wood
where watercress was grown and greenhouses stood,
where a CAT track machine rests on its shovel
like a horse asleep, with loosestrife, tormentil,
wild rhubarb, huge umbellifers,
and held by its neighbours, one fallen conifer.
Think of it creaking in wind, the wrench of its fall
through fists of giant hogweed, and all
the sharp, musk-loaded, insect-shining scent
of earth and air disturbance as it went
down through a lace of elder, thumbs of bracken,
an animal downfall, something stricken
by the weight of winters and history
at the turning of twenty centuries.

Breathing

Prowl the house sniffing out gas leaks,
a cloth festering somewhere,
spilt milk, cat-piss, drains.

Such talent needs exercise.
Putting the cat out, inhale her musk
as she pours herself into the night

like your long ago mother, her fur, her Chanel Number 5,
before the whiff of a moonlighting fox,
and frost, and the coats in the hall.

Some smells are faint, the distinct breath
of tap water from each place you have lived,
the twig of witch hazel two rooms away.

Some are stolen like honey, the secretive salts
of skin, in Waterstone's, say, or the bank,
as you lean together, breathing.

Or the new-born that smell like the sea
and the darkness we came from, that gasp
of the drowned in a breaking wave.

On the Train

Cradled through England between flooded fields
rocking, rocking the rails, my head-phones on,
the black box of my Walkman on the table.
Hot tea trembles in its plastic cup.
I'm thinking of you waking in our bed
thinking of me on the train. Too soon to phone.

The radio speaks in the suburbs, in commuter towns,
in cars unloading children at school gates,
is silenced in dark parkways down the line
before locks click and footprints track the frost
and trains slide out of stations in the dawn
dreaming their way towards the blazing bone-ship.

The Vodaphone you are calling
may have been switched off.
Please call later. And calling later,
calling later their phones ring in the rubble
and in the rubble of suburban kitchens
the wolves howl into silent telephones.

I phone. No answer. Where are you now?
The train moves homeward through the morning.
Tonight I'll be home safe, but talk to me, please.
Pick up the phone. Today I'm tolerant
of mobiles. Let them say it. I'll say it too.
Darling, I'm on the train.

Making the Beds for the Dead

Ewe

MARCH 2003

No. No money in it. Just this:
the two of us in the field's corner
at the crowning,

to feel the heat of it,
to be here at the continuum,
birth and baptismal,

as where rivers meet
and join and go their way,
keeping to themselves

for a while, cold, whole,
even as they empty themselves
into the great mouth of the sea.

Wethers

Spring-born, their lives lived
on the one slope, in the one flock.
Summer, they forget their mothers,
forget our hands, learn grass,

grow wild, wander afield on the hill.
Winter, they know us again, grow tame,
calling for hay at the gate.

At two years, or three,
in winter they walk to death,
silent but for the muffled drums
of their slipshod feet on the road.
In the yard Dai Esger quiets
each one with voice and hand,
before the gun.

Each death is a silence.
Quicker done,
one by one,
than the rabbit
in the cat's jaws,
than the long going out
of our bedridden suffering old.

Quicker than the flock
tumbrelled down the motorway,
fleece to fleece in the tiered truck
rocking the road, sipping drips
from oil-slicked rain on the slats,
then blood and blunder
in a strange country.

Virus

You have to admire its beauty,
its will to live,
fizzing in a soup of chemicals,
wanting nothing but a living host
to practise symmetry
and cell division.

Brought from space
on the heel of a star,
a primitive chemical
seething in soupy pools,
its arithmetic heart
bent on sub-division, multiplication.

On screen, an image
of rotational symmetry
in a box of glass,
a spaceman tumbling
in a two-fold turn,
weightless in his hurtling ship.

Or still life,
computer generated,
a dandelion head, each seed a field,
folding, unfolding flower
smaller than a bacterium,
butting blind towards the living cell.

So where did it start?
Somewhere hot and far away
where they don't fill in forms
to take a sheep to market,
don't call a beast a product,
a commodity.

Where they kill a lamb with a knife at its throat,
and God who loves the lilies of the field
and the one lamb which is lost,
forgot this one with her little,
clicking, cloven, high-heeled hooves,
the horizon in her golden eye.

Rumour

Wool on the wire.
Wind in the gate.
Traed a genau.
Foot and mouth.
The virus on the move
like whispers.

The builder saying:
'There are people
getting rich on this',
as he scrubs,
and changes his boots in the van.

Every farm fortified
by a prickly thicket
of straw at the gate,
buckets and a brush
to dip your boots,
to wash your wheels,
to scour your soul.

The word's on the run,
on the phone.
An anonymous stranger
to a friend of a friend
tried again trading
traed a genau
in a layby on the M4.

For the compensation,
to get out now
while the going's bad.
Say the whispers,
say signs on the gate
traed a genau.

Marsh Fritillary

This could get out of hand,
shake settled things,
rival the good life and the way things are,
shifting the very ground
beneath our feet.

Take Devil's Bit Scabious and the Marsh Fritillary,
interdependent and inseparable
in perfect balance, a flower, a butterfly
among the scabious on Cors Llawr Cwrt,
in the richest colony in Europe.

Each quivering insect turning on its toes
is the double mirror of itself,
in the melt-water of glaciers, where time has spent
an ice age and what followed making right
a scrape of land for a flower and a butterfly.

Fox

SEPTEMBER 2001

First foot in the night fields
down river, across border,
after feasting with crows
on the carcass of a sheep.

Little cat-dog gorged on flesh.
What she can't eat she stashes
in her dozen larders
against hard times.

On the farm track she laps rain
from a cloven pool,
leaving cells to multiply
in the soup of a hoof print.

Sunrise, and the cattle
come home for milking,
slowly, heavily picking their way,
rolling their oiled machinery,

all angles and corners,
old leather toolbags
of hammers and saws,
shoulders and shanks.

On the track they pause
in the footfall of the sun
for a snatch of grass,
a sip from the chalice.

Shepherd

Christmas, and over the snow
a jet chases the day,
cresting the sill of the land
to take the Atlantic.

In the fields
a man and his dog
check the sheep dawn and dusk
as they've always done.

What's it to him,
the flight of kings,
but to remind him
that the world turns,

that going home is a prayer,
that even war draws breath.

Aftermath

The moon stares at the desert,
the dust and the detritus,
the nuzzling warhead,

at the earth's shudder,
dust settling
on a shaken world,

lights the road for the lost,
the footloose, the fugitive,
the warriors and the wounded,

lays linen on the fields,
on beasts asleep on their shadows
in the silver breath of the night,

looks into wind-crumpled water
at the cold bone of its face,
strikes gold in a pond

where the otter has left
two prints, and the peeled skull
of a frog, like the husk of a planet.

Flood

When all's said
and done
if civilisation drowns
the last colour to go
will be gold –
the light on a glass,
the prow of a gondola,
the name on a rosewood piano
as silence engulfs it,

and first to return
to a waterlogged world,
the rivers slipping out to sea,
the cities steaming,
will be gold,
one dip from Bellini's brush,
feathers of angels,
Cinquecento nativities,
and all that follows.

First Words

The alphabet of a house – air,
breath, the creak of the stair.
Downstairs the grown-ups' hullabaloo,
or their hush as you fall asleep.

You're learning the language: the steel slab
of a syllable dropped at the docks; the two-beat word
of the Breaksea lightship; the golden sentence
of a train crossing the viaduct.

Later, at Fforest, all the words are new.
You are your grandmother's Cariad, not Darling.
Tide and current are *llanw, lli*.
The waves repeat their *ll-ll-ll* on sand.

Over the sea the starlings come in paragraphs.
She tells you a tale of a girl and a bird,
reading it off the tide in lines of longhand
that scatter to bits on the shore.

The sea turns its pages, speaking in tongues.
The stories are yours, and you are the story.
And before you know it you'll know what comes
from air and breath and off the page is all

you'll want, like the sea's jewels in your hand,
and the soft mutations of sea washing on sand.

A Pocket Dictionary

'Geiriadur Llogell Cymraeg a Saesoneg', 1861

Fifty years. His handwriting, his name, address.
*Richards' Pocket Dictionary.*1861.
My father's fingerprints. Mine over his.
I look up a word, as I've so often done,
without a thought beyond the page, the word.
Now syllables flock like a whirr of redwings
over the field of my mind. Here the world
began, and then is now. I am searching
for definitions, ambiguities, way
down through the strata, topsoil, rubble,
a band of clay, an inch or so of gravel,
for a particular carbon-dated day,
a seepage in the earth, a gleam of meaning,
a sudden uprise of remembering.

Not

My mother, child of a tenant farm,
learned her place from the landlord's man,
his word 'Welsh' snapped, cutting, curt,
a word that called her 'stranger'.

So my mother would not say the word,
but spat it out like a curse,
a bitterness to be rid of,
to be scoured from her mouth.

My mother's word didn't sound
like the name for a people,
for 'us', for belonging,
for a language older than legend;

or like Nain on the farm, tucking me in
with a prayer and 'Nos da, Cariad',
or calling the hens in the morning, her voice
all cluck and chuckle like scattering corn;

or my father passing the time with stories
as we drove to the sea, teaching me words,
the 'gw' and 'w' of wind and water,
the *ll-ll-ll* of waves on the shore.

Otter

Little water-dog. They almost caught her –
the surface closing over
as the sounding rings of a splash
smashed the moonlit water.

It made its mark on the shore –
paw-print of an otter
and the peeled skull of a frog
just after the slaughter.

Frog caught on the quiet, quartered,
till the skull was a moon
as silvery clean as a spoon
but colder, whiter.

Father and daughter
heard the frog cry 'Broga. Broga.'
Then 'Dŵr. Dŵr,' said water
as it swallowed the otter.

The Fox and the Girl

Once her father came home with a fox cub
in his coat pocket. Lost in the city,
shivering in rubbish outside the pub,
the colour of conkers and as pretty

as a puppy, its teeth like needles.
It hissed in her arms, but she wheedled
to keep it. When it bit her she cried
for her bloody hand, and she cried

when he said, 'Mae'n wyllt. It's a wild
animal, not a pet for a child.'
She could feel its life, its warm fur,
its quick heart beating against her,

and she hurt for its animal mystery,
for the vanishing story of a girl
and a fox lost for words
in the secret forest.

Nettles

for Edward Thomas

No old machinery, no tangled chains
of a harrow locked in rust and rising grasses,
nor the fallen stones of ancient habitation
where nettles feed on what we leave behind.
Nothing but a careless compost heap
warmed to a simmer of sickly pungency,
lawn clippings we never moved, but meant to,

and can't, now, because nettles have moved in,
and it's your human words inhabit this.
And, closer, look! The stems lean with the weight,
the young of peacock butterflies, just hatched,
their glittering black spines and spots of pearl.
And I want to say to the dead, look what a poet sings
to life: the bite of nettles, caterpillars, wings.

A Recipe for Water

Fifty feet down
water flows in the dark.
Rains that spent history
seeping page by page
through the strata,

run black in the aquifers
to rise bringing their gift,
the formula like a spell,
a gulp of cold that flares
at the touch of light.

Calcium, Magnesium, Potassium, Sodium,
Chloride, Sulphate, Nitrate, Iron.

Sip this, the poetry of stone,
a mineral Latin in our blood, our bone.

White

After the theatre, stirred by song and story,
we watch the winter stars from the balcony.

Twelve floors down, two ice-floes in
flux on flow. Each candela

is a mute swan asleep, as white, as luminous
on the black waters of the bay as ice.

Stilled at the edge of the Severn's turbulence
and the tangled waters of two river currents,

their whiteness the definition of lumen,
swans paired for life, a cob and his pen,

wings and necks folded in one dream,
and all the colours of white, which only seem,

Sujata, the very opposite of the blackness
of your black squirrel in Caracas,

but are the same, the one
white rainbow, black, one spectrum.

*

All the spare light in the world is stored
in the folded wings of a pair of sleeping swans,

all the world's spare water stacked miles deep
in the waking ice of the glacier.

The last star dissolves at the lost edge of the moon
afloat on blue like Arctic ice, loosening.

*

At last a change in the weather.
Frost gives up its grip,
ice eases in the bones of trees.
There is movement in the air,
the Atlantic on the wind's breath,
a touch of rain beginning.

A Barge on the Severn

after a painting by Colin Jones (1928–1967)

Where river becomes estuary
before losing its name to the sea,
in water angled by a harbour wall,
on the tilt of the tide's rise and fall
between mudflats, saltmarsh and flood plain,
a boat with the sea in its lap, or rain.

He could have put the river to bed,
baled out the barge, drowned to its gunwale
in flood, in the hope of letting it float.
But he caught the hour and held it,
the cruciform spars of the stern where light
and a salt wind off the channel

still make its lost sail snap in a cross wind,
and the colours brought home in his mind
– red flaking and faded to rose,
and the blue-green of water – have held
forty years, while he, the barge, a particular
hour, timbers, molecules, pigment, particles,

are swept with the soils and silts of Pumlumon
to become the Severn.

Source

After hours plodding uphill in something between
rain and an Atlantic haar, we have come to this:
two thousand feet above the Irish Sea,
a pane of ice, and a muscle of pooling water,

Pumlumon, where five rivers rise, a squelch
of tussocky bog, and the cairn, Garn-fach Bugeilyn,
where story tells us Cai and Bedwyr stood
'in the highest wind in the world'.

We witness a birth, uncertain of what is born,
though we see it's alive, its pulsing placenta,
Hafren, Sabrina, gurgling out of the earth,
headwaters of a stream that will augment

to a headlong hurtling force ready to swallow
Vyrnwy, Stour, Teme, Avon, Afon and Wye,
to bring mountain waters to lap at the thresholds
of cities, to bear off the dead, to shove its way

through limestone in the gorge at Ironbridge,
to be fluent under bridges, to open its hands
letting its multiple muscular waters spread,
to become the estuary, to be lost in the sea.

Sabrina

'There is a gentle nymph not far from hence
That with moist curb sways the smooth Severn stream.
Sabrina is her name, a virgin pure'
                                        — Milton, 'Comus'

Before history there was mythology
fingerprinted between the strata of story
is the human sign. We make a guess
at who they were, and where and why it was.
How the daughter of faithless Locrinus drowned
between an Ice Age and the Age of Stone
to become the river-goddess, a curb in the river.
Today in these fast waters you might glimpse
in the sway of the currents the white limbs
of a girl caught in a shoal of silvers
turning and turning in the turbulence
among migrating salmon, sewin, elvers,
lampreys, eels taking their ancient water-roads
under the shadows of homing birds.

Ice

stopped the throat of the Severn
in the last Ice Age.
so it slept three thousand years,
locked in a frozen lake,

thawed slowly,
built power
beyond Wenlock Edge,
turned south-east,

forced a six mile gorge through rock
at Ironbridge, let loose
the coal, iron, limestone, clay,
that would change the world.

Tide

Lured by the very thought of it, forty-nine feet,
the second highest rise and fall in the world.
Some mornings full to the brim, it slapped and curled
over the prom, and by evening was so far out
you couldn't tell sea from pools, pebbles, mudflats,
wet acres of seaweed, shells, old rope, bird-bones,
fishing lines hooked in the silt, worm-casts, stones,
streams of ebbing water flashing with light.
Once, on a strange beach, the Severn turned on us.
It surged thundering up the steep sand,
carried and cast us ashore like detritus
then tried to drag us back on retreating waters,
as when the sea-king stole the old man's daughters.

Bore

The sea charges in
against the outpour
of a big, bold river,
no holds barred.

So a water-dragon is born.
A self-powering soliton
heaves upstream,
rearing its crested head,

past cathedrals, towns,
a seven foot wave
rolling up-country
where no wave should be.

It rips out river banks,
nudges a stone from the stanchion
of a bridge,
sweeps footpaths away,

carries off cars,
the carcass of a sheep,
tons of old red sandstone,
and surfers hitching a ride.

Migrations

Signals
between a weather satellite
wavering among the steady stars
and seven swans tagged with transmitters,
asleep on a lake in southern Finland.

First light. Bewick's and Whooper swans
wheel off the water, beating west,
the Russian Arctic tundra out of mind,
their future the washy estuaries
of Severn, Dyfi, Neb or Ouse.

It's nothing new, on wing, on foot,
the hungry take to the roads of a restless earth,
in flight from famine, slaughter, war,
on ancient journeys across seas, deserts,
across the latitudes and longitudes.

But this is new, intimate, tracking
the secret flight of a Bewick's swan,
its heartbeat in my hand
as it homes a thousand miles,
to winter on wetlands in Wales.

I fly with it, imagining space
beating with luminous wings:
satellites, angels, souls,
the seven ghosts of Concorde
blowing the firmament,

the world's roads dark
with human travellers,
each caravan of hunger
a mythic journey to an inn,
in want of shelter, water, bread.

Glacier

The miles-deep Greenland glacier's lost its grip,
sliding nine miles a year towards the sea
on its own melt-water. As, forty years ago,
the slag-heap, loosened by a slip
of rain-swollen mountain streams, suddenly
gave with a roar, a down-hurtling flow
of spoil taking a primary school.
crushing the children. The century of waste
has burned a hole in the sky over the Pole.
Oh, science, with your tricks and alchemies,
chain the glacier with sun and wind and tide,
rebuild the gates of ice, halt melt and slide,
freeze the seas, stay the floe and the flux
for footfall of polar bear and Arctic fox.

Coins

Stalled in Kingsway traffic, engine idle,
watching for peacocks and the grey friar's ghost,
I remember the diving boys, the water-course lost
under the hum and cumber, the old canal

scuttling in its culvert, covert, echoing
slaps of rat-shadow and the shout
of marble boys, or boys as brown as trout,
their skinny shoulder blades like broken wings.

They dived for pennies from the parapet
a life ago, falling through green light
with a gasp, to surface, blowing water,
shaking their otter heads, coins bright

on their palms. Down there in the filth and cold
lies, dated like a journal, my lost gold.

Llandâf Cathedral

Before the saints, Dyfrig, Teilo, Eiddogwy;
before the bishops, the builders and stonemasons;
before artists and sculptors, Rossetti, Epstein;
before music, organists and choirs;
before architects, Jasper Tudor, Wood, Seddon, Prichard, Pace;
before the poetry of psalm and hymn and common prayer;

before 'cathedral', 'architecture', 'art',
when our first house
was the great original forest,
when our ancestors walked in the aisles of trees
and gazed up into the loftiness, confused,
perhaps, by inexplicable longing;

before there was a word for wonder,
or names for stars, or footprints on the moon,
before Saint Teilo raised his church just here,
before a man looked at a tree and made a cross,
and felt the hammering rain and thought of nails,
there must have been a first creative act,

first mark, first word, first hymn to awe,
first poem with something to say of the human heart,
first vision of a building taller than the forest,
aisled, vaulted, clerestoried with sunlight, imagined
into being, because we were forest-dwellers once
and learned our metaphors from trees.

A Sonnet for Nye

London was used to trouble from the Valleys,
People who lived close, loved song and word,
Despised the big men's promises and lies.
With them the socialist vision struck a chord.
Colliers, who hated class and privilege,
Whose work was filthy, dark and perilous,
Spared a portion of their paltry wage
To pay a stricken neighbour's doctor's bills.
They sent their man to Parliament. Who dares
Wins. A fierce man with a silver tongue,
He hammered stammered words in the hallowed air
Of the House, an Olympian among them,
Stuttering his preposterous social dream
Translated from 'a little local scheme'.

Mercury

What tows it back tonight?
A bead of silver rolling among the stars,
and a jet's growl trailing behind its light.

One distant afternoon, the house in a drowse
between Hoovers and teatime, I creep in,
open his desk, slide out the drawers.

Caught from the broken barometer, harm
caged in a tobacco tin, humming, glamorous,
loose and luminous as a swarm.

The thought of it still shivers in the bone,
how it breaks into beads then shoals at the tilt of the tin.
Dangerous quicksilver. I'm alone,

while the grown-ups nap in their rooms.
Nothing to do but open things, touch the forbidden,
the whole, slow, summer afternoon.

It could get under your skin, electricity
running your veins, nerves, bones.
It could light you up like a city.

A trick of the night sky and I'm there again, taking
a tiger out of a drawer, my promise, the law,
silence, his trust, my heart, all of it breaking.

Bach at St Davids

for Elin Manahan Thomas

In spring, fifteen centuries ago,
the age of saints, and stones, and holy wells,
a blackbird sang its oratorio
in the fan-vaulted canopy of the trees,
before Bach, before walls, before bells,
cantatas, choirs, cloisters, clerestories.
The audience holds its breath when the soprano,
like a bird in the forest long ago,
sings the great cathedral into being,
and apse to nave it calls back, echoing,
till orchestra and choir in harmony
break on the stones like the sea.
And listen! Out there, at the edge of spring,
among the trees, a blackbird answering.

Wings

I wake suddenly in the night
to feel the moon's glaciers
slide their silvers over the bed
engulfing the two of us,

and touch you to be sure, scared
at the silence between the phrasing
of a breath, your shoulder cold,
your moonlit hand marble.

The early hours. I listen, lift my head
to lose the muffle of feathers,
the crack of inter-stellar static,
the knock of my own heart

and yours, beating steadily over the tundra,
paired for life, migrating through the night
in falling feathers of snow, your shoulder blades
warm again, wingless, human.

Old Libraries

Shelved quietly out of sight and mind,
The dog-eared, the foxed, the uncut, unread,
The sagging, slipped, asleep, inclined
On the shoulders of stiff volumes no one reads.
Pressed between their pages, wedding flowers,
Fingerprints, last will and testament,
Letters of longing, love, condolence,
A final note before the long descent
From a bridge over black water
Far from home in someone else's town.
And maybe once the scarcely legible lines
Of longhand like veins on the crumpled wings
Of the emerging moth, a lost sonnet soars
On one unfolded wing to the world's applause.

Advent

Dark times. December.
Earth's axis on the slant
and the minutes fall from the day
a few at a time.

So we outsleep the dark,
sleepwalking the grey hours.
Impossible to believe in light,
or a birth, until

this winter sunrise, fox
going home with blood in its mouth,
all the dawn's chemicals in its eye,
and the sky astonished.

Dawn

A dark swish of starlings
like curtains parting
in a hushed auditorium

and the show begins:
a bowl of fire in a beech tree,
then earth and sky suffused in flame.

This could be the first dawn,
the world brand new,
just out of its wrapper,

sky a great window open
a moment only
in the east,

giving a glimpse of the myth
before the first footprint,
before the fall.

Polar

Snowlight and sunlight, the lake glacial.
Too bright to open my eyes
in the dazzle and doze
of a distant January afternoon.

It's long ago and the house naps in the plush silence
of a house asleep, like absence,
I'm dreaming on the white bear's shoulder,
paddling the slow hours, my fingers in his fur.

His eyes are glass, each hair a needle of light.
He's pegged by his claws to the floor like a shirt on the line.
He is a soul. He is what death is. He is transparency,
a loosening floe on the sea.

But I want him alive.
I want him fierce
with belly and breath and growl and beating heart,
I want him dangerous,

I want to follow him over the snows
between the immaculate earth and now,
between the silence and the shot that rang
over the ice at the top of the globe,

when the map of the earth was something we knew by heart,
and they had not shot the bear,
had not loosed the ice,
had not, had not . . .

Ice

Where beech cast off her clothes
frost has got its knives out.

This is the chemistry of ice,
the stitchwork, the embroidery,
the froth and the flummery.

Light joins in. It has a point to make
about haloes and glories,
spectra and reflection.

It reflects on its own miracle,
the first imagined day
when the dark was blown

and there was light.

River

As if on its way to the sea
the river grew heavy,
a knife of pain in its heart,
slowed, slewed to a halt,

words slurred in its mouth
frozen in a dream of death,
came to, foot on the clutch,
engine running.

Struck dumb,
in a curb of ice
stilled in its sleep
under a hail of stars.

Where a river barge cuts upstream
in aching cold the surface cracks.
The drowned stir in their dream
as boat and boatman pass.

The shoals lie low,
silvers of elver, salmon like stones.
The backwash cuts the floe
to spars and bones,

the brimming ribcage
of a drowned beast.

Snow

We're brought to our senses, awake
to the black and whiteness of world.
Snow's sensational. It tastes
of ice and fire. Hold a handful of cold.

Ball it between your palms
to throw at the moon. Relish its plushy creak.
Shake blossoms from chestnut and beech,
gather its laundered linen in your arms.

A twig of witch hazel from the ghost-garden
burns like myrrh in this room. Listen!
Ice is whispering. Night darkens,
the mercury falls in the glass, glistening.

Motorways muffled in silence, lorries stranded
like dead birds, airports closed, trains trackless.
White paws lope the river on plates of ice
in the city's bewildered wilderness.

White Nights

In the luminous pages of the night,
under the deep drift of the duvet,
that silence like the world gone deaf.

In clouds of cold our bedroom holds its breath
like wartime winters. Roads unmake themselves
across a trackless land caught in the Mabinogi.

I'm wakeful, stalled by a stuttering line of verse.
By dawn, the garden hasn't stirred. Not a breath
shakes off the snow. Trees stand like death,

locked in that cold wedding in the story,
house, fields, in forever's frozen air.
Day after day the wait, weighted, bridal.

This is what Marged knew under this roof,
thatched then, I suppose, a hundred years ago,
quilt and carthen* weighing her bones like stone,

hay-dust, cold, the sickness in her lungs, the knell
of the cow lowing to be milked, kicking its stall,
lamp and stove to light, on her last winter dawn.

---

* *carthen*: a traditional Welsh blanket

Freeze 1947

Long ago in the first white world, school closed.
The park disappeared, the lake froze,
the town lost its way, sea struck dumb
on the beach. Birds held their tongues.

Land lay spellbound. World was an ice garden
beyond fern-frozen glass. Trees held out white arms,
waltzed with the wind and froze to stone.
On doorsteps bottled milk stood stunned.

The polar bear rug on the living room floor
rose from the dead, shook snow from its fur
and stood magnificent on all fours,
transfigured, breathing flowers.

And a girl on the road from school was stolen, her breath
a frozen rose, her marble sleep, death.
They hid the paper. 'Babe in the Wood' it said.
I thought of her school desk, its name-carved lid

slammed on slurred air, her face blurred
over books her eyes of ice would never read,
her china inkwell emptied of its words,
the groove for her pen like a shallow grave.

Swans

She was brave in the bitter river,
the *Mary Rose*, doomed,
ice-chalice, lily in bloom.

Thaw, her feathers and bones dissolve in the flow
and she's gone, flower that floated
so light over death's undertow.

In lengthening light he patrols alone
ferocious on his watery shore
where the nest from last year and the year before

has drowned to a dredge of sticks and sludge.
In full sail, his body ablaze, bridge
over unfenced water, he waits for her.

The voice on the phone said,
'He doesn't know she's dead.
There is nothing to be done.'

Now love rides the river
like a king's ship, all wake and quiver,
and I can't tell him, it's over.

Who Killed the Swan?

'She is mine,' said the river
holding the swan on its palm like a lily.

Said the sky, 'She is mine to have and to hold,
my small white cloud of cold.'

'She is mine,' sighed the wind, wounding the air,
winnowing water, lifting a wing.

'Mine,' said the sun, noosing the swan
with a cold gold ring.

The cob swims in silence, its neck a question,
head downcast over water's mirror.

He lifts archangel wings to scorch the sky,
churning water and wind to rise

above the river, beating alone upstream.
'She is beside me, my soul, my dream,

the current under my heart.
Where I fly, she flies beneath me.'

Thaw

Tonight the river's on the move
in a lovely backstroke, taking the tide
with a kick of silk thighs, shoulders

heaving the flood through flux
and fluency, stroking the keels
of coot and mallard, a single swan,

rocking a flock of gulls on its palm,
coupling grebe, boats at their mooring,
on currents swollen with melt
of mountain snows.

Fluent

Sleek as a girl in her silk, kissing goodnight
before slipping out to the dance, she'd leave her scent
on my pillow, the warmth of her skin on my cheek.
Cold pooled in the satin folds of her dress,
the glint of her rings, her animal wrap of fur,

and she's gone, night-river slipping its chains,
fluent, reflective, pulling to sea
under winter's weight, freighted
with ruin and wrack, a burden of birds, words
dead and alive, trees, driftwood, plastic,

and all my lost mountain syllables sing
on her frozen, loosening tongue
remembered, remembering.

Nant Mill

as if her broken words were scattered stones,
each course of the house unmade like a thought unspoken;
as if the walls, ruined in rampant sycamore,
were a language lost to a mumble of elder and bramble,
her story erased by too much silence;

as if she stood beside me checking the place
against the photograph – the field-gate at the bend
where the lane disappears, the cornerstone of the door
here where they stood, stilled on the threshold
in a new century before the wars;

as if the gap in the wall over the river
still held the butter churn, its paddle turning
where the current is slow with a secret dark,
then out with a shining song across the ford
where the horse's hooves once scattered water like sparks;

as if she left home one day, no turning back
and nothing to say; as if she might whisper again
the words for water, horse, mill, stream –
dŵr, ceffyl, melin, nant – in the tongue
the Clywedog has always sung.

Burnet Moths

We walk the old dog on Grangemoor hill
raised on a city's waste, the filth of landfill.
Her tail's a flag of joy waving through grasses,
a blur of butterflies, larksong, and all the pleasure
a generous day can give to human and dog
walking a meadow nourished on trash and decay.

By the path, bound to grass stems, spindles of spit,
chrysalids, papery, golden, torn, unfurling
sails of damp creased silk, spinnakers filling
with breath, burnet moth wings of scarlet and black
like opera stars who live and love and die
in an hour on the flight of an aria.

Now it's her turn to die, her beautiful head on my knee,
her life an infinity still, till the sedative takes,
and she crumples to sleep at my feet, folded back
to before she was born. The kind vet waits.
Sleep isn't death. Then the needle, barbiturate
straight to the heart. Here – and gone.

Er Gwell, Er Gwaeth[1]

a'r fodrwy hon y'th briodaf[2]. . .
Something about the ring in the blackbird's eye
on an April evening; the raptor's jewelled stare;
the marriage of sun and rain on dancing water;
the circle of my arms round sheets off the line;
yours bringing armfuls of wood for the fire.

â'm corff y'th anrhydeddaf[3]. . .
Something of touch, taste, tongue, the language
of hands, those chemical gifts one to the other;
grace and gesture, silence, reflection,
that pair for life two swans on a river
soundlessly sculling the stream, lover to lover.

â'm holl olud bydol y'th gynnysgaeddaf[4] . . .
My dowry a derelict house on a hill, five fields,
two acres of bluebells under oaks; yours, a vision.
You made sound the ruin, dreamed space and light,
a room of oak and glass, let in the sky, the hills,
and all of Ceredigion, *Cariad[5]*, in a glance.

---

[1] *Er Gwell, Er Gwaeth*: For Better, For Worse
[2] *a'r fodrwy hon y'th briodaf*: with this ring I thee wed
[3] *â'm corff y'th anrhydeddaf*: with my body I thee worship
[4] *â'm holl olud bydol y'th gynnysgaeddaf*: with all my worldly goods I thee endow
[5] *Cariad*: darling

Running Away to the Sea — 1955

It might have been heatstroke, the unfocused flame of desire
for a name in a book, a face on the screen, the anonymous
object of love. Two schoolgirls running like wildfire,
bunking off through dunes to the sea, breathless.

We were lost and free, East of Eden.
It was James Dean, Elvis, Bill Haley and the Comets.
It was Heartbreak Hotel on the gramophone.
It was Heathcliff by torchlight in bed after lights-out.

The dunes were molten glass. We slowed to a dawdle,
rippling sand with our toes, grains of gold
through our fingers, on our skin, in our hair,
without words to say why, or who, or where.

This I remember. The hour was still, bees
browsing sea lavender, and beyond the dunes
the channel as blue as the Gulf of Araby,
a name from the drowse of a daydreaming lesson,

sun on the board, the chalk, Sister's hand, a far-away
voice, as if heard through water, murmuring rosaries:
Egypt, the Red Sea, the Bitter Lakes, Suez.
A psalm of biblical names called Geography.

That was the last day the world stood still. In a year
there'd be tanks in Budapest, over Sinai bombers on the move,
and I'd be in the streets on the march against war,
as empires loosened their grip. It was almost like love.

Oradour, 10 June 1944

Silence in the empty streets, the square,
the shuttered houses, sun-blind boulangerie,
dressmaker, surgery, school, Mairie.

At the oil-clothed table in the shade of a vine,
Madame Roufanche is pouring a rough red wine,
ladling cassoulet into yellow bowls,
with a crusty cheese, an armful of warm loaves
brought home that morning, the dew still
on the fields, her quilt like a cloud on the sill.

We could have been here, passing through, like now,
could have risen, restored, in love, from the bed
in the room overlooking the square, could have shared
her table, her man home from work, a nod, nothing said,
could have talked in French, in smiles, in gesturing hands,
in the raise and ring of glasses, the breaking of bread.

That long ago summer the house, the church, the dead
in their graves, the streets, the square, all spread
under the linen of silence, sunlight, noon,
waiting for boots, orders, the struck match, the gun,
the church full of women fired, men in the burning barn,
and safe in the future, we and our love not born.

Six Bells

*for the forty-four miners killed in
the explosion on 28 June 1960*

Perhaps a woman hanging out the wash
paused, hearing something, a sudden hush,

a pulse inside the earth like a blow to the heart,
holding in her arms the wet weight

of her wedding sheets, his shirts. Perhaps
heads lifted from the work of scrubbing steps,

hands stilled from wringing rainbows onto slate,
while below the town, deep in the pit

a rock-fall struck a spark from steel, and fired
the void, punched through the mine a fist

of blazing firedamp. As they died,
perhaps a silence, before sirens cried,

before the people gathered in the street,
before she'd finished hanging out her sheets.

Blue Hydrangeas

You bring them in, a trug of thundercloud,
neglected in long grass and the sulk
of a wet summer. Now a weight of wet silk
in my arms like her blue dress, a load

of night-inks shaken from their hair –
her hair a flame, a shadow against light
as long ago she leaned to kiss goodnight
when downstairs was a bright elsewhere

like a lost bush of blue hydrangeas.
You found them, lovely, silky, dangerous,
their lapis lazulis, their indigos
tidemarked and freckled with the rose

of death, beautiful in decline.
I touch my mother's skin. Touch mine.

The March

for my late father-in-law, Glyndwr Thomas,
miner, Oakdale colliery

Boots and rain drummed the tram roads,
that bitter night in 1839,
potholed and stumbled with mud and stones.
Five thousand men, workers in iron and coal
from mine and furnace, Sirhowy, Ebbw, Rhymni,
heads bowed against the storm like mountain ponies.

Their bones ached from the shift, wind in the shaft,
the heat of the furnaces. Yet on they marched,
their minds ablaze because their cause was right,
through darkness from Ebbw Vale, Blackwood, Pontypool,
faces frozen and stung by the lash of rain,
trudging the roads to Newport through the night.

At the Welsh Oak, Rogerstone, betrayed by daylight,
Frost's men from the west, Williams's from the east,
Jones's men never arrived. The rest struck on
to stand, single-hearted in the square
before the Westgate. Had they stood silent then,
had they not surged forward, had not been shaken

by rage against injustice, had they muzzled
the soldiers' muskets with a multitude
of silence, had reason spoken,
those steely thousands might have won the day.
But they stormed the doors to set their comrades free,
and shots were fired, and freedom's dream was broken.

A score dead. Fifty wounded. Their leaders tried,
condemned, transported. The movement, in disarray,
lost fifty years. Then came at last that shift
of power, one spoonful of thin gruel at a time,
from strong to weak, from rich to poor,
from men to women, like a grudged gift.

The Year's Midnight

The flown, the fallen,
the golden ones,
the deciduous dead, all gone
to ground, to dust, to sand,
borne on the shoulders of the wind.

Listen! They are whispering
now while the world talks,
and the ice melts,
and the seas rise.
Look at the trees!

Every leaf-scar is a bud
expecting a future.
The earth speaks in parables.
The burning bush. The rainbow.
Promises. Promises.